Bruce's
Bakery Cookbook

Facing
up to
Bruce's
cakes

Bakery eatery
knows recipes
for success

ROBIN LEACH

BRUCE....

Baker to
the Stars

Bruce's Bakery Cookbook

Recipes from the Famed New York Eatery

BRUCE ZIPES

Clarkson Potter/Publishers
New York

In memory of my dad, Harry, for always having the patience to teach
me and the time to love me

And for my daughter Ryann and my son Jared, the little loves of my
life, for being the official taste-testers and always "telling it like it is"

Published by Clarkson Potter/Publishers, New York, New York.
Member of the Crown Publishing Group.

Random House, Inc. New York, Toronto, London, Sydney, Auckland
www.randomhouse.com

CLARKSON N. POTTER is a trademark and POTTER and colophon
are registered trademarks of Random House, Inc.

Printed in the United States of America

Design by Maggie Hinders

Library of Congress Cataloging-in-Publication Data
Zipes, Bruce.
Bruce's Bakery cookbook / Bruce Zipes—1st ed.
1. Desserts.   I. Bruce's Bakery (N.Y.)   II. Title.
TX773.Z56 2000
641.8'65—dc21   00-020901

ISBN 0-609-60474-0

10   9   8   7   6   5   4   3   2   1

First Edition

Acknowledgments

My sincere thanks go to a number of people who assisted in the writing and preparation of this book:

First and foremost, my heartfelt thanks to my partner, Joel Goldberg, my alter ego for fifteen beautiful years together. Thanks, too, to my agent, Noah Lukeman, for making it possible to transform an idea into a reality. And to Margot Schupf, my editor at Clarkson Potter, for her thoughtful shepherding of the book through the various phases of the publishing process. A big thank-you to my recipe editor, Trish Shoemaker, who expertly adapted the bakery recipes for the home kitchen, and to writer-editor Karen Berman, who helped tell this baker's story. Finally, I thank the wonderful staff at Bruce's, both in the bakery and the restaurant; without you, we couldn't pull it off day after day. And thanks to our loyal customers and to the community of Great Neck, New York, for your patronage, and for being demanding and always keeping us on our toes.

Contents

Introduction

Some of my earliest memories involve working at my father's bakery. I was seven years old and he would send me out to make deliveries. I'd get on the bus, clutching my parcel of bread or rolls or marble cake, and when I got to the customer's building, I'd ride the elevator to the right floor, drop off the package, and if I was lucky (which I usually was), I'd get a quarter as a tip.

My father, Harry, brought me with him to the bakery every weekend. I don't know if it was because he wanted to spend time with me or to teach me the business—probably a little of both. But I loved those Saturdays at the bakery and I've loved every day of the baking business since. Baking is a creative art and a precise science all at the same time. You feed people's stomachs and their souls. I'm lucky enough to get to do that every day at Bruce's, in the beautiful community of Great Neck, Long Island. Customers sometimes ask me how I do this or that; people don't bake at home the way they used to. But I've found that when they taste something delicious, something that Grandma or Great-Grandma might have made, they get curious and want to see if they can do it, too. And so, after forty-plus years in the business (remember, I really did start when I was seven), I've decided to set down what I've learned about baking. The result is this book.

I'm a third-generation baker. My maternal grandfather, Izzy, came to this country around the turn of the century from Russia or Poland. (The borders of those countries kept changing in those years and even he was never quite sure which!) He settled in Brooklyn and had a successful bakery there. Izzy taught his son-in-law the baking business, and in a few years Harry had a chain of eighteen bakeries all over Manhattan called the Lorri Barrie, the third largest in the city.

The flagship store was located at the corner of 89th Street and Broadway, and sometimes it seemed like the whole world passed through its doors. Ed Sullivan used to drop in and so did bandleader Eddie Duchin. Babe Ruth lived at 89th Street and Riverside Drive, and he came into the store every morning. My father used to say he didn't know if the Babe was just waking up or just getting home. He and my dad were friends for years.

When I was fourteen, Harry sold the Lorri Barrie chain. He called himself semi-retired, but he opened a bakery on Long Island, where we had settled when we moved from Brooklyn a few years before. I worked in the bakery on weekends, preparing racks of jelly doughnuts, making coffee cakes and chocolate-dipped cookies—whatever needed to be done. I learned by experience and sometimes by making mistakes. I remember the first time I ever made chocolate icing. I put the ingredients into a pot over an open flame. As anyone who has ever worked with icing knows, sugar has a low burning point, so you need a medium flame and a double boiler. My flame was too hot and I put my pot over direct heat. Instead of getting a nice rich icing at what we call "blood temperature," I got burnt sugar. Not realizing this, I proceeded to ice three racks of doughnuts. When I finally did figure out what I had done, I not only had to remake the icing, but rebake all the doughnuts and re-ice them, too. That was a lesson that has served me ever since: Understand your ingredients.

Harry was a wonderful teacher and he was patient. He was an exacting baker; he taught me never to take shortcuts and never to use cheap ingredients. (He wouldn't have dreamed of using shortening in a recipe that called for butter!) He shared with me every aspect of running a bakery, not just the baking end, but the business end as well. And he had a wonderful personality. Everybody knew him by his first name. People loved him, and of course I did, too. He died in 1988. I miss him; without him, his guidance, I would not be as successful as I am today.

I worked in my father's bakery all through high school. If he took a week off to go on vacation, I'd take the week off from school to mind the store. After high school, I attended Hofstra University, where I majored in advertising and marketing, working in my father's bakery the whole time. When I graduated, I decided to open a bakery of my own. A bakery and café followed, but I had always wanted to do a bakery and restaurant combination. In 1984, I got a chance to do just that.

I had met my partner Joel Goldberg when he was managing a local restaurant near my bakery. Harry and I stopped in for dinner after work one day and Joel was there. He was always very attentive to all his customers. In fact, I noticed that he was a lot like me—he insisted on the best quality and the most conscientious service. He had grown up in the food business in much the same way that I had in the bakery business. He likes to say that he was born in a pickle barrel; his father had a successful pickle business in—small world!—Brooklyn. We had grown up within blocks of each other but had never met before. He, too, had worked with his father, getting up at four or five in the morning to set up the pickle stand in all kinds of weather. And like me, he had moved to Long Island.

It turned out that he had been dreaming of a bakery-restaurant combination just like me, so we decided to go into business together. It was a beautiful relationship from the get-go. We opened Bruce's in Great Neck on May 10, 1984, at six o'clock in the morning. From the start, we established a custom of serving every table in the restaurant a complimentary plate of freshly baked rolls, mini muffins, danish, coffee cake, and pastries from the bakery. Our customers loved it, and after their meals, they'd stroll over to the bakery counter to buy baked goods to take home. Or they'd buy their baked goods and then sit down for breakfast, lunch, or dinner. We always gave our restaurant patrons a little doggie bag so they could take home the leftovers from their bakery plates; they loved that. Business was good, and ten years later, we bought our own building and expanded to twice our original size. In 1997, we opened a branch of Bruce's at First Avenue and 57th Street in Manhattan.

We have customers who have been with us since we opened; we've catered their weddings, their anniversaries, bar mitzvahs, and graduation parties. We do special orders; some of our most successful permanent menu items have resulted from individual requests from customers. Like both our fathers, Joel and I insist on serving only the highest quality merchandise. We've built our reputation on that, and we know that we owe our success to a customer base that appreciates what we can deliver. We're grateful for their support, and we try to do as much as we can to give back to the community.

So when charity auctions need cakes, we donate them. When a congregation needs baked goods for a special event, we supply them. We've helped the Great Neck Arts Center and the Long Island Jewish Medical Center, the Make-A-Wish Foundation and Ronald McDonald House. We donated a complete brunch to 400 cancer survivors on Cancer Survivors' Day at Long Island Jewish Medical Center; Joel's family has unfortunately been touched by cancer, and we wanted to support those who are beating the disease. When the Gulf War was over, we gave a full dinner, free of charge, for 100 local veterans and their spouses; we just wanted to do something for them. If we do a good deed, we don't expect anything in return, but I must say that we were thrilled when, in 1997, we received the Giraffe Award, Great Neck's most prestigious honor for community service. A letter from President George Bush hangs in a place of honor in the restaurant: "You are to be commended for your spirit and deep involvement in your community—our nation thrives on civic pride."

We also like to have fun—and we've built a bit of a reputation for that, too. For several years, Joel and I hosted a TV talk show right from the restaurant, *Breakfast at Bruce's,* which was broadcast via the local cable access channel. We interviewed everyone—from the late actor Vincent Gardenia to baseball great Whitey Ford. I've appeared on network television shows numerous times—and my cakes have been featured as well. We've been featured on *Live with Regis and Kathie Lee, The Today Show,* Rosie O'Donnell, Rikki Lake, Montel Williams, Joe Franklin, John Stewart, CBS, NBC, ABC, and local news. Once the cast of *All My Children* took over our kitchens for a plot line that involved a bakery. Naturally, we baked some treats for them to take when they left.

We've also become known for a sideline that developed a number of years ago: portrait look-alike cakes. The Westbury Music Fair, a major Long Island center for the performing arts, contacted us to bake a birthday cake for Bob Hope, who was appearing there. They wanted to do something special and we decided we were going to put Hope's face on the cake. Using a photo of Hope, one of our staffers "painted" it freehand. It was such a good likeness that the folks at Westbury asked us to present it to Hope. From then on, we did cakes for just about everybody who appeared there, and our slogan became "Bruce's: Baker to the Stars." Joe Piscopo abandoned his diet and exercise program long enough to consume the entire cake himself after a show at Westbury. Kathie Lee Gifford liked our work so much she ordered an engagement cake for a segment she was doing on her TV show shortly before her marriage to Frank Gifford. We've created cakes for Regis Philbin, Jay Leno, Julio Iglesias, Cindy Crawford, Bill Cosby, Howie Mandel, Dr. Ruth Westheimer, Joan Rivers, Robin Leach, Katie Couric, Matt Lauer, Al Roker, Liberace, Dinah Shore, Christie Brinkley, and Wayne Newton, to name a few. Visitors to Bruce's have included Leah Thompson, Howard Stern, Lou Diamond-Phillips, and Hillary Clinton.

I even brought cakes for Whitey Ford and Mickey Mantle to spring training in Florida. I went to the Yankees' fantasy camp in Florida for four years in a row, and each time I brought an assortment of pastries and coffee cakes for the team in my carry-on luggage; later in the week, Joel would ship down fresh reinforcements. I got to play ball with all my heroes; besides Mantle and Ford, there were Moose Skowkron, Ron Gidrey, Hank Bauer, Catfish Hunter, and others. And they got to taste our baked goods. Whitey Ford, who lives in the area, became a regular customer.

Everywhere I travel, I meet people who know Bruce's. They all tell me the same thing: "You should open a Bruce's near my house." It makes me happy to hear that they like what we do, but it makes me sad, too, because it means that they don't have a bakery like Bruce's where they live. It used to be that there were two or three family bakeries in every town. Now there are two or three towns—or more—for every family bakery. Running an independent bakery is a demanding business, and there's a lot of competition from the chains, the supermarkets, the coffee places—you name it. At this point in history, it's not exactly a growth industry. Sometimes I feel like I'm the last living dinosaur. Which is why, I guess, I wanted to write this book, to set down these wonderful recipes, so that people who don't have an old-fashioned family bakery nearby can create their favorites for themselves. So here are my treasures—some of them passed down to me from my grandfather and my father—for you to bake in your own kitchen. Enjoy.

Basic Ingredients

BUTTER

I bake exclusively with unsalted or sweet butter, a baking basic I learned from my father, who would always say, "Salted butter is too salty to use in baking." Salt, which acts as a preservative, also masks butter that is not fresh. Some recipes specify that butter be softened before you incorporate it into the batter. Pay close attention and plan ahead; soften butter at room temperature. Sometimes, when creaming butter and sugar, the mixture will look curdled. A baker's trick my father taught me is to add a tablespoon or two of the flour called for in the recipe to the creamed butter/sugar mixture to hold it together; this will also help when you add the dry ingredients. Always store butter in an airtight container, as it absorbs odor rapidly.

CHOCOLATE

The recipes in this book mainly use dark chocolate, also known as semisweet, bittersweet, or European-style chocolate. Dark chocolate has a high percentage of cocoa solids—around 75 percent—and is slightly sweetened with sugar. Semisweet chocolate is generally sweeter than bittersweet. The rich, intense flavor and deep color of dark chocolate make it ideal for desserts and cakes. Working with chocolate over the years, I have found there is an enormous difference in both texture and flavor among brands, and have developed my own personal preferences. I recommend you do the same.

I find melting chocolate the traditional way—over a double boiler—is best. Place the coarsely chopped chocolate in the top of a double boiler over hot (not simmering, not boiling) water. Melt the chocolate, stirring until smooth. Do not cover the bowl of chocolate while it is melting. You might remove the chocolate from the heat just before it is completely melted, as it will continue to melt on its own. Warning: Chocolate is a delicate substance that requires patience and care; too much heat, and you'll wind up with a scorched mess.

CINNAMON

Cinnamon, by far the most popular dessert spice, is the inner bark of a tropical evergreen tree. When the bark is dried, it curls into quills. The quills are sold as cinnamon sticks or ground into powder. Once I thought all cinnamon tasted the same. Not true. I prefer the *Cinnamomum cassia* from Saigon, which has a very sweet essence.

CREAM

Use heavy whipping cream, which contains 36 to 40 percent butterfat. It will be pasteurized, but avoid creams that are labeled "ultrapasteurized." This commercial process increases its shelf life, but ultrapasteurized cream does not whip as well as other cream. To speed up the process, use a chilled bowl and chilled beaters when whipping cream. In fact, in the summertime I place the chilled bowl in a larger bowl of ice to keep it really cold.

EGGS

All the recipes in this book were tested with grade A large eggs. Whether the eggs have brown or white shells makes no difference, but make sure you buy eggs as fresh as possible, so look for a market with high turnover. For all baking, but especially yeast baking, do not use eggs straight from the refrigerator. In general, eggs must be brought to room temperature before using. If you haven't had a chance to let your eggs sit at room temperature for 20 minutes on the counter to warm, put them in a bowl (still in their shells), cover them with warm water for 1 or 2 minutes, then drain.

FLOUR

Most of the recipes in this book call for all-purpose flour. It may be either bleached or unbleached. The difference between the two is that bleached flour has undergone a chemical process that makes it appear whiter than unbleached flour. The bleaching process does compromise some of the nutrients, but they are often added back to the flour. I've found that the recipes work well using either.

In bread recipes I use bread flour, which contains more gluten and protein than all-purpose flour. Rye flour is a traditional ingredient in many cakes and pastries of Northern and Eastern Europe. Because of its distinct flavor, it works well, but is usually combined with cake flour or all-purpose flour because alone it doesn't have sufficient gluten to provide the right amount of elasticity. Cake flour, milled from soft winter wheat, does not contain gluten; it is more refined than all-purpose flour and produces a tender, delicate crumb. I prefer it for chiffon cakes. Some cake flour is self-rising, which means baking powder and salt are incorporated into the flour. I do not use self-rising cake flour in any of the recipes in the book.

HONEY

For baking, I use an amber-colored New York State buckwheat honey, which is mild enough to harmonize with the other ingredients. If you can't find buckwheat honey, amber clover honey will make a good substitute. To minimize crystallization, honey should be stored in an airtight container in a cool place or in the refrigerator for long-term storage. If it does crystallize, place the jar of honey in a saucepan of hot water and heat until the crystals have liquefied.

LEAVENERS

For the recipes in this book, I used "double acting" baking powder, a chemical leavener. It's called double acting because it works twice; once when it comes in contact with liquid and again when it comes in contact with heat. My father always warned me, "Use only fresh baking powder." Baking powder should be replaced every four to six months. To test for freshness, add a teaspoon of baking powder to about 4 ounces of hot water. If it bubbles, the powder is still good. I am always amazed at the extra volume a cake will have when made with fresh baking powder.

Baking soda, also a chemical leavener, is an ingredient that turns up in preparations featuring acidic ingredients such as yogurt, orange juice, sour cream, or buttermilk. It will only react in the presence of an acid and is usually used in conjunction with baking powder. Baking soda is said to have an indefinite shelf life, but I feel that since it absorbs odors from the air, it's a good idea to replace it every three months or so.

NUTS

It is crucial that nuts used in baking be fresh. Nuts can turn rancid rather quickly, walnuts and pecans more so than almonds. Always smell and taste nuts before using them—you will know quickly if they are rancid. If you even suspect they might be, do not use them; they will ruin your recipe. For walnuts, I use the English or Italian varieties, which originally came from Europe and are now grown in California. Something else I learned from my father Harry: Use only amber-colored or light walnuts; the lighter the walnut, the sweeter it is. Stay away from dark walnuts with black spots, a sign they are old. Nuts can be stored in the freezer, well wrapped, for several months.

SUGAR

In this book, when the recipe calls for sugar, I'm referring to the granulated or superfine varieties. Superfine sugar is granulated sugar that has been processed to reduce the size of the grains. Confectioners', or powdered, sugar is granulated sugar that has been milled to a fine powder and then mixed with cornstarch to prevent lumping. Always sift confectioners' sugar before using.

As for brown sugar, mostly as a matter of personal taste, I use light brown sugar in all my recipes, although dark brown, which has a rich molasses flavor, will work just as well. Unless otherwise stated in the recipe, always pack brown sugar firmly into a dry measure so it holds the shape of the cup when turned out.

VANILLA AND OTHER EXTRACTS

If you are using vanilla from the supermarket shelves, buy only the finest, purest products available. For better flavor, buy those labeled "pure extract" instead of "imitation," which does not taste nearly as good and gives you only minimal cost savings. Of the gourmet varieties of vanilla, I like Madagascar Bourbon and Tahitian. Extracts lose potency when exposed to light, so store them in a cool, dark cupboard and make sure that the tops are always tightly closed.

Basic Equipment

BAKEWARE

Bakeware is made in a range of materials: aluminum, tin, stainless steel, black steel, ceramic, and glass. I have found that I get the best results with glass and dark or dull-finish bakeware. The dark or dull finish absorbs more heat, increasing the amount of browning, which will yield all kinds of benefits: heavier cake crusts, piecrusts that are evenly browned underneath as well as on top, crisp and nicely browned bread crusts, and crisper cookies.

CAKE COMB

You really get a professional look if you use a serrated comb to finish the sides of layer cakes. Combs come in metal or plastic, are available in various sizes, and are sold in kitchen supply stores.

COOLING RACKS

Cooling racks work well for cooling baked goods, both in and out of the pan, because they allow for full air circulation around the cake or pastry. I also like them for glazing because they allow excess glaze to drip off the cake, creating a clean bottom edge.

ELECTRIC MIXERS

Mixers are a baker's best friend. Handheld electric mixers and heavy-duty standing mixers both work well to blend most cake batters and cookie doughs. Portable handheld electric mixers are perfect for short mixing periods and light jobs such as beating egg whites or whipping cream. They can be used with nearly any bowl. For heavy-duty jobs and long mixing periods, a freestanding electric mixer works best, and it leaves you free to proceed with another part of the recipe. Standing mixers are equipped with their own bowls.

LONG SERRATED KNIFE

A long serrated knife is ideal for slicing a cake on the horizontal and also good for chopping chocolate. A good-quality stainless or carbon steel knife will last a lifetime, but it's not necessary to buy the most expensive one on the market.

MEASURING EQUIPMENT

It's important to have separate equipment for solid and liquid measures to ensure that you're measuring ingredients accurately. A good kitchen supply store will carry measuring equipment for both solids and liquids, and the staff there should be able to help you to make selections that suit your needs.

PASTRY BAG

Pastry bags are bags designed to hold frosting or other decorating materials for piping onto cakes and confections. They're fitted with removable tips whose openings have various shapes and sizes depending on the design desired. They're available commercially in various sizes in nylon, plastic, or plastic-coated cotton. After you use them, rinse and dry them thoroughly. If you don't have a pastry bag and tip, for simpler jobs like drizzling chocolate, spoon the melted chocolate into a small plastic bag and, using scissors, snip the end of one corner. Gently squeeze the chocolate through the hole to create any design you wish. Start with the smallest hole you can and adjust the hole if necessary after a few practice squeezes—you can make it bigger if you need to, but you can't make it smaller. Or make your own pastry-decorating cones out of parchment paper triangles fastened on the out-side with tape.

ROLLING PINS

When choosing the proper rolling pin, getting one to fit your hands is most important. Heavy, high-quality smooth wooden rolling pins are best for working with piecrusts and other dough. The heavier the rolling pin is, the better it will perform. I prefer French-style rolling pins, which taper at the ends and have no handles. For fine pastry work, marble rolling pins are recommended because they stay cool and don't raise the temperature of the dough despite the friction that rolling creates. Wooden rolling pins should never be submerged in water, but you should always, always wipe them with a damp cloth and rub them dry with a kitchen towel.

SPATULAS

Rubber spatulas are important for folding and mixing batters as well as scraping down the sides of the bowl. They are produced flat-sided or in a concave, spoonlike shape, and are available in rubber or heat-resistant silicone. It's a good idea to have several.

A metal spatula with a narrow blade and a wooden handle is the best tool for frosting cakes. A ten-inch metal spatula works for spreading frosting on top of layers, while a smaller eight-inch spatula works well for frosting the sides of layer cakes.

TURNTABLE

Frosting cakes is so much easier if you have a turntable, a pedestal approximately five inches tall, with a rotating top. An inexpensive plastic lazy Susan works as well as a heavyweight footed variety.

Cheesecakes, Pound Cakes, and Tea Cakes

Banana Cake

*O*ver the years, we've found that the best banana cakes are made from overripe bananas—the blacker the banana, the sweeter and more flavorful the cake. To speed the ripening process, place the bananas in a paper or plastic bag or fruit-ripening bowl. As my partner Joel says, "A mature banana is a good banana." So if your bananas are getting soft and mushy, don't run for the garbage disposal; instead, preheat the oven.

2½ CUPS ALL-PURPOSE FLOUR

2 TEASPOONS BAKING POWDER

1 TEASPOON SALT

1 TEASPOON BAKING SODA

1 CUP (2 STICKS) UNSALTED BUTTER, SOFTENED

1½ CUPS SUGAR

3 EGGS

1 TEASPOON VANILLA EXTRACT

1¾ CUPS MASHED OR PUREED RIPE BANANAS
(ABOUT 3 TO 4 MEDIUM-SIZE BANANAS)

2 CUPS CHOPPED WALNUTS (OPTIONAL)

CONFECTIONERS' SUGAR, FOR DUSTING

Preheat the oven to 350° F. Grease and flour an 8½-inch Bundt pan.

In a large bowl, sift together the flour, baking powder, salt, and baking soda; set aside.

In a large mixing bowl, cream the butter and sugar together until light and fluffy. Add the eggs, one at a time, beating well after each addition. Add the vanilla and mashed bananas. Add the flour mixture and mix until combined. Stir in the walnuts, if using.

Pour the batter into the prepared pan and bake for 55 to 60 minutes, or until a toothpick inserted in the center comes out clean. Cool in the pan on a wire rack for 10 minutes, then remove from the pan and cool completely.

To serve, dust with sifted confectioners' sugar.

SERVES 12

Danish Tea Cake

Hans *was a baker from the Netherlands who worked in my father's bakery for years. He taught us how to make this Old World cake, which has become a favorite at Bruce's. Brown sugar is the principal sweetener, and the layer of pecans on top gives the cake an extra measure of elegance. It's delicious alone or served with a warm fruit compote.*

1/4 CUP WHOLE PECANS

3 CUPS CAKE FLOUR

1 TEASPOON BAKING POWDER

1/2 TEASPOON SALT

1/2 TEASPOON BAKING SODA

1²/3 CUPS FIRMLY PACKED LIGHT BROWN SUGAR

2 EGGS

3/4 CUP VEGETABLE OIL

1 TABLESPOON VANILLA EXTRACT

1 CUP SOUR CREAM

CONFECTIONERS' SUGAR, FOR DUSTING

Preheat the oven to 350°F. Grease and flour an 8½-inch Bundt pan. Place the pecans in the bottom of the pan and set aside.

In a large mixing bowl, combine the flour, baking powder, salt, and baking soda.

In another mixing bowl, combine the brown sugar, eggs, oil, ½ cup water, and the vanilla, and beat until well blended. Gently add the flour mixture, beating for 1 to 2 minutes until well blended. Add the sour cream and mix well. Pour the batter into the prepared pan.

Bake for 50 to 60 minutes, or until a toothpick inserted near the center comes out clean. Cool on a wire rack for 10 minutes. Remove from the pan and cool completely.

To serve, dust with sifted confectioners' sugar.

SERVES 12

New York Cheesecake

I didn't have much time for getting into trouble when I was a kid because I was always helping my dad in his bakery. But I was—and am—a New York kid, tough and proud. My partner Joel says I was the toughest baker in Brooklyn. And I'll put my melt-in-your-mouth New York cheesecake with its sweet cookie crust up against anyone's. It's the best, simple as that, and the orders we get to ship it all over the country prove the point.

Cookie Crust

1 CUP ALL-PURPOSE FLOUR

1/4 TEASPOON SUGAR

1 TEASPOON GRATED LEMON ZEST

1/2 CUP (1 STICK) UNSALTED BUTTER,
     CUT INTO SMALL PIECES AND CHILLED

1 EGG YOLK, LIGHTLY BEATEN

1/4 TEASPOON VANILLA EXTRACT

Filling

5 8-OUNCE PACKAGES CREAM CHEESE, SOFTENED

1 3/4 CUPS SUGAR

1/4 TEASPOON SALT

1/2 TEASPOON VANILLA EXTRACT

5 EGGS

2 EGG YOLKS

1/2 CUP SOUR CREAM

Preheat the oven to 375° F.

To prepare the crust, in a large bowl, combine the flour, sugar, and lemon zest. Using a pastry blender or two knives, cut in the butter until the mixture is crumbly. Using a fork, stir in the egg yolk and vanilla until all the dough is moistened.

Pat one third of the crust over the bottom of a 9-inch springform pan with its sides removed. Bake for about 6 to 8 minutes, or until golden brown. Cool. Grease the sides of the springform pan and attach to the bottom. Pat the remaining two thirds of the crust around the sides, coming up to a height of about 2 inches.

Increase the oven temperature to 475° F. In a large mixing bowl at medium speed, beat together the cream cheese, sugar, and salt until creamy. Add the vanilla. Add the eggs and egg yolks, one at a time, beating well after each addition. Add the sour cream and mix well. Pour the mixture into the prepared crust.

Bake for 10 minutes. Watch the top of the cake to avoid overbrowning. Reduce the oven temperature to 200° F. and bake for an additional 60 minutes.

Transfer the pan to a wire rack to cool slightly, about 10 minutes. While the cake is still warm, gently run a thin-bladed knife around the inside edges of the pan to loosen the sides of the cake. When completely cool, carefully remove the sides of the pan. Chill for at least 2 hours before serving.

SERVES 12

California Cheesecake

¶ *developed this cheesecake after a visit to my sister Shelly in California, where everybody obsesses about fat and calories. During my stay I sampled "light" cheesecake at a bakery in Beverly Hills. I was skeptical at first: Would a lighter cheesecake be any good? To my surprise, it was, and I spent the flight home ruminating on how I could recreate it in my bakery. This is the result. Beaten egg whites and low-fat cottage cheese reduce the fat without sacrificing texture or taste. Served with fresh berries, it makes a spectacular dessert for summer—or any season.*

Chocolate Crust

1¼ CUPS FINELY CRUSHED CHOCOLATE WAFER CRUMBS
   (ABOUT 40 WAFERS)

4 TABLESPOONS (½ STICK) UNSALTED BUTTER, MELTED

Filling

3 CUPS 1% LOW-FAT COTTAGE CHEESE (1 24-OUNCE CONTAINER)

2 8-OUNCE PACKAGES CREAM CHEESE, SOFTENED

1 CUP PLUS 2 TABLESPOONS SUGAR

1 TEASPOON VANILLA EXTRACT

½ TEASPOON GRATED LEMON ZEST

2 EGGS

4 EGG WHITES

¼ TEASPOON CREAM OF TARTAR

SLICED FRESH STRAWBERRIES

FRESH BLUEBERRIES

Preheat the oven to 325°F.

In a small bowl, combine the chocolate wafer crumbs and butter. Press the mixture into the bottom of an ungreased 10-inch springform pan, forming the crust.

In the bowl of a food processor, combine the cottage cheese and cream cheese and blend until smooth. Add ¾ cup of the sugar, the vanilla, lemon zest, and whole eggs and process until smooth. Transfer to a large bowl and set aside.

In a mixing bowl, beat the egg whites and cream of tartar on medium speed until frothy, about 1 minute. Gradually add the remaining 6 tablespoons of sugar, 1 tablespoon at a time, beating on high speed until stiff peaks form. Gently stir one fourth of the egg white mixture into the cream cheese mixture and blend to lighten the batter. Gently fold in the remaining egg white mixture, folding just until combined.

Pour into the prepared crust and bake for 50 to 55 minutes, or until almost set; the cake should still be slightly moist and soft in the center but will become firm as the cake cools. Remove the pan from the oven and cool on a wire rack for 15 minutes. Loosely cover and chill for at least 8 hours before serving.

To serve, carefully run a thin-bladed knife around the inside of the pan to loosen the cake. Remove the pan from the cake and top with fresh berries.

SERVES 12

Chocolate Chocolate Cheesecake

*M*y *partner Joel always says he's never met a cheesecake he didn't like, and believe me he's tasted a few! Being a cheesecake aficionado, he rates this extremely rich and ultra-delicious recipe the best chocolate cheesecake he's ever devoured. For a really creamy filling, make sure all the ingredients are at room temperature before you begin.*

Chocolate Crumb Crust

2 CUPS FINELY CRUSHED CHOCOLATE WAFER CRUMBS
   (ABOUT 40 WAFERS)

6 TABLESPOONS (¾ STICK) UNSALTED BUTTER, MELTED

3 TABLESPOONS SUGAR

Filling

4 8-OUNCE PACKAGES CREAM CHEESE, SOFTENED

¾ CUP PLUS 2 TABLESPOONS SUGAR

2 TABLESPOONS CORNSTARCH

2 EGGS, LIGHTLY BEATEN

1 CUP SOUR CREAM

1 TEASPOON VANILLA EXTRACT

8 OUNCES GOOD-QUALITY SEMISWEET CHOCOLATE, MELTED
   AND COOLED

Preheat the oven to 375° F.

To prepare the crust, in a small bowl, combine the chocolate wafer crumbs, butter, and sugar. Press the mixture firmly into the bottom and 1 inch up the sides of a 9-inch springform pan, forming the crust. Bake for 8 to 10 minutes.

Increase the oven temperature to 450° F.

To prepare the filling, in a large mixing bowl at medium speed, beat together the cream cheese, sugar, and cornstarch until creamy. Add the eggs, one at a time, mixing on low speed and beating well after each addition. Add the sour cream and the vanilla and mix well. Stir in the melted chocolate and pour the mixture into the cooled prepared crust.

Bake for 10 minutes, then reduce the oven temperature to 200° F. and bake for an additional 55 minutes. Turn the oven off and allow the cake to cool in the oven for 3 hours, with the door slightly open.

Remove the cheesecake from the oven and transfer the pan to a wire rack. Gently run a thin-bladed knife around the inside edges of the pan to loosen the sides of the cake. Chill for 4 hours or overnight. When completely cool, carefully remove the sides of the pan.

SERVES 16

˗Flourless Chocolate ˗Torte

¶ *call this superbly creamy torte "chocolate velvet." It was originally developed for Passover because it doesn't require leavening, but it quickly became a year-round favorite with our customers. Try it with vanilla ice cream and come up with your own description!*

½ CUP SUGAR

½ CUP LIGHT CORN SYRUP

10 OUNCES GOOD-QUALITY BITTERSWEET CHOCOLATE,
   COARSELY CHOPPED

½ CUP (1 STICK) UNSALTED BUTTER

5 EGGS

1 RECIPE CHOCOLATE GANACHE (PAGE 145)

Preheat the oven to 350° F. Grease a 9-inch springform pan.

In a small, heavy saucepan, combine the sugar and corn syrup. Cook over low heat, stirring until the sugar is dissolved, about 2 minutes. Remove from the heat.

In another small saucepan, combine the chocolate and butter and cook over low heat, stirring until the chocolate melts. Remove from the heat and add the sugar mixture to the chocolate mixture. Set aside.

In a medium mixing bowl, beat the eggs on high speed until light and fluffy. Reduce the speed to low and add the sugar and chocolate mixture, beating until well combined.

Pour into the prepared pan. Bake for 30 to 40 minutes, or until the cake is puffed and a cake tester or toothpick inserted in the center comes out with moist crumbs. Cool in the pan on a wire rack for 30 minutes. Carefully run a thin-bladed knife around the inside edges of the pan to loosen the cake. Remove the sides of the pan and let cool completely. Wrap the cake in plastic and chill for at least 4 hours before frosting.

Remove the cake from the refrigerator and remove the plastic wrap. Place the cake on a wire rack set over a baking sheet. Using a metal spatula, spread the Chocolate Ganache evenly over the top and sides of the cake. Refrigerate the cake for 10 to 15 minutes to set the ganache.

SERVES 12

Golden Pound Cake

*T*his pound cake recipe has been in my family for three generations. Years ago, my father Harry sold it as a wholesale item, and it was served in almost every coffee shop in New York. I don't think it's an exaggeration to say it set the standard for pound cake in the city. You can do as the restaurants used to do and top it with ice cream, fresh berries, or hot fudge—or all three. Or skip the fuss, because this tender, moist cake can easily stand alone.

1½ CUPS (3 STICKS) UNSALTED BUTTER, SOFTENED

1 1-POUND PACKAGE CONFECTIONERS' SUGAR
(APPROXIMATELY 3¾ CUPS)

6 LARGE EGGS, AT ROOM TEMPERATURE

1 TEASPOON VANILLA EXTRACT

3 CUPS ALL-PURPOSE FLOUR

1½ TEASPOONS BAKING POWDER

¾ TEASPOON SALT

½ CUP MILK

CONFECTIONERS' SUGAR, FOR DUSTING

Preheat the oven to 325°F. Lightly grease and flour a 10-inch tube pan.

In a large mixing bowl, beat the butter with an electric mixer on medium speed for about 30 seconds, until smooth. Reduce the speed to low and gradually add the sugar, beating until well combined. Increase the speed to high and beat until light and fluffy, about 8 minutes.

With the mixer still on high, add the eggs, one at a time, beating well after each addition. Continue beating, scraping down the sides of the bowl once or twice, until the mixture is smooth and very pale and has increased in volume, about 7 minutes. Beat in the vanilla.

In a medium bowl, combine the flour, baking powder, and salt. Gradually add the flour mixture to the batter, alternating with the milk and beating well after each addition until smooth.

Scrape the batter into the prepared pan and use the back of a spoon to even out the surface. Bake for 65 to 75 minutes, or until a toothpick or cake tester inserted in the center comes out clean.

Cool the cake for 30 minutes in the pan, then invert the cake onto a platter and cool completely.

To serve, dust with sifted confectioners' sugar.

SERVES 16

Honey Cake

This is our own special formula for honey cake, developed after years of tinkering and refining. New York State buckwheat honey is my secret ingredient. I love this dark, heavy honey because it has a sweetness unlike any other, but it can be hard to come by. If you can't find buckwheat honey, amber clover honey is a good alternative. All the other ingredients add a little something: The rye flour keeps the cake from being too sweet and the cinnamon, allspice, and orange round out the flavor profile. It's a honey of a cake!

1 CUP VEGETABLE OIL

3 EGGS

1½ CUPS SUGAR

1 CUP HONEY, PREFERABLY BUCKWHEAT OR AMBER CLOVER HONEY

1½ TABLESPOONS GRATED ORANGE ZEST

1½ CUPS RYE FLOUR

1¼ CUPS CAKE FLOUR

2 TEASPOONS BAKING POWDER

½ TEASPOON BAKING SODA

2 TEASPOONS GROUND CINNAMON

½ TEASPOON ALLSPICE

½ TEASPOON SALT

1 CUP ORANGE JUICE

CONFECTIONERS' SUGAR, FOR DUSTING

Preheat the oven to 350° F. Grease and flour a 12-cup Bundt pan.

In a large mixing bowl, beat the oil, eggs, and sugar until blended. Gradually add the honey and orange zest and mix until blended. In another medium bowl, combine the rye flour, cake flour, baking powder, baking soda, cinnamon, allspice, and salt. Add the flour mixture to the egg mixture alternately with the orange juice, beginning and ending with the flour mixture; beat until smooth.

Pour the batter into the prepared pan. Bake for 50 to 55 minutes, or until a toothpick inserted in the center comes out clean. Cool the cake completely on a wire rack.

To serve, dust with sifted confectioners' sugar.

SERVES 16

Marble Cake

The recipe for this marble cake has been in my family for three generations. My grandfather Isadore brought it with him when he came to the United States. Izzy, as everyone called him, was an old-time baker—these days we'd call him a workaholic, but back then he was just struggling to make a living in a new land. Sometimes, though, in the middle of the morning, he'd take a break for coffee—he'd already been at work for at least five hours—and he liked to have a little marble cake too. Almond paste—sweetened ground almonds—gives it an extra kick. If there's none in your pantry, almond paste is available in most supermarkets.

3 OUNCES ALMOND PASTE

1 CUP SUGAR

8 TABLESPOONS (1 STICK) UNSALTED BUTTER, SOFTENED

8 TABLESPOONS VEGETABLE SHORTENING

4 EGGS

4 EGGS, SEPARATED, WHITES AND YOLKS RESERVED

1 TABLESPOON VANILLA EXTRACT

3 CUPS CAKE FLOUR

2 TEASPOONS BAKING POWDER

1 TEASPOON SALT

¼ CUP MILK

8 OUNCES GOOD-QUALITY SEMISWEET CHOCOLATE,
   MELTED AND COOLED

Preheat the oven to 350° F. Generously grease and flour a 12-cup Bundt pan.

Using a grater or a food processor, grate or shred the almond paste into a large mixing bowl.

Add ½ cup of the sugar to the almond paste and cream together, then add the butter and shortening and beat until light and fluffy, about 3 minutes. Blend in the eggs, egg yolks, and vanilla. In another bowl combine the flour, baking powder, and salt. Add the flour mixture to the wet ingredients alternately with the milk, until all the flour and milk are incorporated. Continue beating, scraping down the sides of the bowl once or twice, until the batter is smooth.

In a separate mixing bowl on medium speed, beat the egg whites until soft peaks form. Gradually add the remaining ½ cup sugar and beat until stiff peaks form, about 3 minutes. Using a rubber spatula, gently fold one quarter of the egg whites into the batter to lighten the batter. Fold in the remaining egg whites.

Spoon half of the batter into the prepared pan. Drizzle half of the melted chocolate over the batter and swirl a knife through the batter to marble it. Spoon the remaining cake batter into the pan.

Bake for 45 to 55 minutes, or until a toothpick inserted in the center comes out clean. Cool for 30 minutes in the pan. Carefully run a thin-bladed knife around the inside edges of the pan to loosen the sides of the cake from the pan and invert the cake onto a platter. Drizzle with the remaining melted chocolate.

SERVES 16

Marble Chiffon Cake

When *my father Harry developed heart problems later in life, he started paying more attention to what he ate. This lighter version of marble cake was just what his doctor ordered. The vegetable oil and egg white in the formula reduce the fat content and make the cake moist and tender, while the rich veins of chocolate swirls and glossy chocolate ganache glaze make it as tasty as any traditional marble cake. Be sure to use a vegetable oil that will impart as little flavor as possible, such as soy, corn, safflower, or sunflower oil.*

2¼ CUPS SIFTED CAKE FLOUR

1½ CUPS SUGAR

1 TABLESPOON BAKING POWDER

½ CUP VEGETABLE OIL

7 EGGS, SEPARATED, YOLKS AND WHITES RESERVED

1 TABLESPOON GRATED ORANGE ZEST

1 TEASPOON VANILLA EXTRACT

¾ CUP COLD WATER

½ TEASPOON CREAM OF TARTAR

4 OUNCES GOOD-QUALITY SEMISWEET CHOCOLATE,
  MELTED AND COOLED

1 RECIPE CHOCOLATE GANACHE (PAGE 145)

Preheat the oven to 325° F.

In a large mixing bowl, combine the flour, 1¼ cups of the sugar, and the baking powder. Make a well in the center of the flour mixture and add the oil, egg yolks, orange zest, vanilla, and cold water. Beat on low speed until well combined. Increase the speed to high and beat for an additional 5 minutes, until very smooth.

In a large mixing bowl, beat the egg whites and cream of tartar until soft peaks form, about 2 minutes. Gradually add the remaining ¼ cup of sugar, 1 tablespoon at a time, continuing to beat until stiff peaks form. Gently fold the batter into the egg whites. Pour into an ungreased 10-inch tube pan.

Drizzle the melted chocolate over the cake batter and swirl a knife through the batter to marble it. Bake on the lowest rack in the oven for 65 to 70 minutes, or until the top of the cake springs back when lightly touched. Immediately invert the cake in the pan and cool thoroughly on a wire rack. Carefully run a thin-bladed knife around the inside edges of the pan to loosen the sides of the cake. Transfer the cake to a wire rack set over a baking sheet. Using a metal spatula, spread the Chocolate Ganache evenly over the top and sides of the cake. Refrigerate 10 to 15 minutes to set the ganache.

SERVES 16

Philly Fluff
Bruce's Famous Signature Cake

*M*y *father Harry was constantly trying to make every item in his bakery just a little bit better. It was his mission. In this case, he took a basic pound cake and added extra cream cheese and lots of real butter. The result was a moist, dense, super-rich cake, which has become our signature. It's expensive to make, but it's our best-selling cake. Try it yourself and you'll understand why.*

10 OUNCES CREAM CHEESE, SOFTENED

½ CUP (1 STICK) UNSALTED BUTTER, SOFTENED

½ CUP VEGETABLE SHORTENING

2 CUPS ALL-PURPOSE FLOUR

2 TEASPOONS BAKING POWDER

½ TEASPOON SALT

2 CUPS SUGAR

6 EGGS

1 TEASPOON VANILLA EXTRACT

8 OUNCES GOOD-QUALITY BITTERSWEET CHOCOLATE,
  MELTED AND COOLED

Preheat the oven to 350° F. Grease and flour an 12-cup Bundt pan.

In a large mixing bowl, cream together the cream cheese, butter, and shortening until light and fluffy. In a small mixing bowl, combine the flour, baking powder, and salt. Add the flour mixture to the creamed mixture and mix until blended.

Gradually add 1 cup of the sugar and the eggs, one at a time, beating well after each addition. Add the vanilla and the remaining 1 cup sugar and continue beating, scraping down the sides of the bowl once or twice, until the batter is smooth.

Pour half of the mixture into the prepared pan. Top with half of the melted chocolate and swirl a knife through the batter to marble it. Top with the remaining batter.

Bake for 60 to 65 minutes, or until a toothpick inserted in the center comes out clean. Cool on a wire rack for 15 minutes. Invert the cake onto a platter and cool completely. Before serving, drizzle the cake with the remaining melted chocolate.

SERVES 16

Sour Cream Cake

Whoever says they don't make 'em like they used to hasn't tasted Bruce's sour cream cake. We make it the way my father Harry did, right down to the tempting topping of chocolate, cinnamon, brown sugar, and walnuts.

1 CUP (2 STICKS) UNSALTED BUTTER, SOFTENED

2½ CUPS SUGAR

4 EGGS

1 TABLESPOON VANILLA EXTRACT

4 CUPS ALL-PURPOSE FLOUR

½ TEASPOON SALT

1 TEASPOON BAKING SODA

4 TEASPOONS BAKING POWDER

⅛ TEASPOON GRATED NUTMEG

1¾ CUPS SOUR CREAM

¼ CUP MILK

Chocolate Nut Topping

½ CUP FIRMLY PACKED LIGHT BROWN SUGAR

1 TABLESPOON UNSWEETENED COCOA POWDER

2 TEASPOONS GROUND CINNAMON

½ CUP MINI CHOCOLATE CHIPS

½ CUP FINELY CHOPPED WALNUTS

Preheat the oven to 350° F. Generously grease a 10-inch tube pan. Line the bottom of the pan with parchment paper, and then grease the parchment paper.

In a large mixing bowl, cream together the butter and sugar until light and fluffy. Blend in the eggs and vanilla. In another bowl, combine the flour, salt, baking soda, baking powder, and nutmeg. Fold the flour mixture into the egg mixture, alternating with the sour cream and milk, to make a smooth batter. Continue beating, scraping down the sides of the bowl once or twice, until the mixture is smooth, about 2 minutes.

In a small bowl, combine the brown sugar, cocoa powder, cinnamon, chocolate chips, and walnuts. Spoon half of the batter into the prepared pan. Sprinkle with 1 cup of the chocolate nut mixture. Top with the remaining batter. Sprinkle with the remaining chocolate nut mixture.

Bake for 60 to 70 minutes, or until the top is slightly crusty. Cool for 30 minutes in the pan. Carefully run a thin-bladed knife around the inside edges of the pan to loosen the sides of the cake before removing to a platter. Cool completely.

SERVES 16

Chocolate Melt-Away Coffee Cake

At the Bruce's Bakeries in Great Neck and Manhattan, the Chocolate Melt-Away Coffee Cake is one of the first to disappear off the shelf. If you come too late, you won't get one. Now everyone calls in advance to reserve their Melt-Away. This coffeecake is best served warm from the oven, which is a great excuse to dive into it without having to wait until it cools.

Topping

8 OUNCES GOOD-QUALITY SEMISWEET CHOCOLATE, COARSELY CHOPPED

3/4 CUP CHOPPED PECANS

2/3 CUP FIRMLY PACKED LIGHT BROWN SUGAR

Cake

2½ CUPS ALL-PURPOSE FLOUR

2½ TEASPOONS BAKING POWDER

1 TEASPOON BAKING SODA

½ TEASPOON SALT

½ TEASPOON GROUND CINNAMON

3/4 CUP (1½ STICKS) UNSALTED BUTTER, SOFTENED

1¼ CUPS SUGAR

3 EGGS

1½ CUPS SOUR CREAM

2 TEASPOONS VANILLA EXTRACT

Preheat the oven to 350°F. Grease a 12-cup Bundt pan.

In a small bowl, combine the chocolate, pecans, and light brown sugar and set aside.

In a medium-size bowl, combine the flour, baking powder, baking soda, salt, and the cinnamon and set aside.

In large mixing bowl, beat the butter and sugar until light and fluffy. Add the eggs, one at a time, beating well after each addition. Add the sour cream and vanilla and mix well. Add the flour mixture and mix on low until well combined.

Spoon one-third (about 2 cups) of the batter into the prepared pan, spreading evenly. Sprinkle with one-third of the topping (about 1 cup). Repeat the layering process two more times. Bake for 55 to 65 minutes, or until a toothpick inserted in the center comes out clean. Cool in the pan on a wire rack for 20 minutes, then remove from the pan and cool completely.

SERVES 12

Chocolate Roulade with White Chocolate Mousse Filling

At the bakery we wanted to expand our line of cakes without adding another layer cake. So voilà! The Chocolate Roulade was born. This particularly indulgent dessert is a light and delicate chocolate sponge filled with rich white chocolate mousse then glazed with ganache. Use a good imported white chocolate for this. Most of the American ones are made with vegetable shortening instead of cocoa butter, which really gives chocolate its flavor.

Chocolate Sponge Cake

4 EGGS, SEPARATED, YOLKS AND WHITES RESERVED

½ TEASPOON VANILLA EXTRACT

¾ CUP SUGAR

⅓ CUP ALL-PURPOSE FLOUR

¼ CUP UNSWEETENED COCOA POWDER

1 TABLESPOON BAKING POWDER

¼ TEASPOON SALT

White Chocolate Mousse Filling

6 OUNCES GOOD-QUALITY WHITE CHOCOLATE, FINELY CHOPPED

6 TABLESPOONS (¾ STICK) UNSALTED BUTTER, CUT INTO ½-INCH SQUARES

½ CUP CONFECTIONERS' SUGAR

6 TABLESPOONS HEAVY CREAM

1 RECIPE CHOCOLATE GANACHE (PAGE 145)

Preheat the oven to 375° F. Line the bottom of a 15½ × 10½-inch jelly-roll pan with parchment or wax paper. Grease the paper and the sides of the pan and lightly dust with flour.

To prepare the sponge cake, in a mixing bowl, beat the egg yolks on high speed for about 5 minutes until thick and lemon-colored. Add the vanilla. Reduce the speed to low and gradually beat in ¼ cup sugar. Continue beating until the mixture thickens slightly and doubles in volume, about 5 minutes.

In a small bowl, sift together the flour, cocoa, baking powder, and salt. Sift ⅓ cup of the flour mixture over the egg yolk mixture and gently fold it in until combined. Repeat with ⅓-cup measures of the remaining flour mixture until it is all incorporated.

In a mixing bowl, beat the egg whites on medium speed until soft peaks form, about 2 minutes. Gradually add the remaining ½ cup sugar to the egg whites, beating on high until stiff peaks form. Gently fold 1 cup of the beaten egg white mixture into the egg yolk mixture to lighten the batter, then fold the whole yolk mixture into the egg white mixture. Pour into the prepared pan.

Bake for 12 to 15 minutes, or until the cake springs back when lightly touched. Cool on a wire rack for 10 minutes. Run a thin-bladed knife around the edge of the cake to loosen the sides.

Turn the cake out onto a towel sprinkled with confectioners' sugar. Gently peel off the parchment paper and roll up the towel and the cake, jelly-roll style, starting from a long side. Place on a wire rack and cool completely.

To prepare the filling, in a small saucepan over medium heat, melt the white chocolate and butter. Remove from the heat and stir in the confectioners' sugar.

continued on next page

In a mixing bowl, whip the cream until soft peaks form. Over low speed, add the white chocolate mixture and combine well. Allow the filling to cool, stirring occasionally until it begins to stiffen.

Carefully unroll the cake and trim the edges with a serrated knife. Using a spatula, spread the white chocolate mousse filling over the surface of the cake to within 1 inch of the edges. Use the towel to re-roll the cake compactly; trim the ends with a serrated knife. Wrap the cake roll in aluminum foil and refrigerate for 2 hours, or until firm.

Unwrap the cake roll and place it on a wire rack set over a baking sheet. Using a metal spatula, spread the Chocolate Ganache evenly over the top and sides of the cake roll. Refrigerate for 10 to 15 minutes to set the ganache.

SERVES 10

Layer Cakes

Blackout Cake

*A*ll the bakeries in Brooklyn used to make blackout cake. My father's bakery made the best, of course, and this is his version: chocolate cake, rich chocolate pudding, and chocolate crumb coating. At Bruce's, we use chocolate cake crumbs for the outer coating, but cookie crumbs work well, too. To make the cookie crumbs, break cookies into chunks and place between two pieces of wax paper or wrap them in a clean kitchen towel and roll firmly with a rolling pin. My partner Joel appointed himself the official Blackout Cake Taste-Tester. It's a tough job, but somebody's got to do it.

Chocolate Layer Cake

6 EGGS, SEPARATED, YOLKS AND WHITES RESERVED

1 TEASPOON VANILLA EXTRACT

1¼ CUPS SUGAR

½ CUP CAKE FLOUR

½ CUP UNSWEETENED COCOA POWDER

1 TEASPOON BAKING POWDER

6 TABLESPOONS (¾ STICK) UNSALTED BUTTER, MELTED

½ TEASPOON CREAM OF TARTAR

1 RECIPE BLACKOUT CREAM (PAGE 132)

2 CUPS CRUSHED CHOCOLATE WAFER CRUMBS
   (ABOUT 40 CHOCOLATE WAFERS)

Preheat the oven to 350° F. Grease and flour a 9-inch springform pan. Line the bottom of the pan with parchment paper or wax paper. Grease the paper and set aside.

In a mixing bowl, beat the egg yolks on high speed about 5 minutes, or until thick and lemon colored. Add the vanilla. Reduce the speed to low and gradually beat in 1 cup of the sugar. Continue beating until the mixture thickens slightly and doubles in volume, about 5 minutes.

In a small bowl, combine the cake flour, cocoa, and baking powder. Sift ⅓ cup of the flour mixture over the egg yolk mixture and fold it in until combined. Repeat with ⅓-cup measures of the remaining flour mixture until it is all incorporated. Blend in the butter.

In a mixing bowl, beat the egg whites and cream of tartar on medium speed until soft peaks form, about 2 minutes. Gradually add the remaining ¼ cup of sugar to the egg whites, beating on high speed until stiff peaks form. Gently fold 1 cup of the beaten egg white mixture into the egg yolk mixture to lighten the batter, then fold the whole yolk mixture into the egg white mixture. Pour into the prepared pan.

Bake for 30 to 35 minutes, or until the cake springs back when lightly touched. Cool on a wire rack for 10 minutes. Remove the pan and cool completely.

Cut the cake in half horizontally, forming 2 equal layers. Place one layer on a serving plate and spread with Blackout Cream. Top with the remaining cake layer. Frost the top and sides with the remaining Blackout Cream. Sprinkle the cake with the chocolate wafer crumbs.

SERVES 12

Carrot Cake with
Cream Cheese Frosting

This cake has been a best-seller for my family for three generations, which only proves that when something's really good, it's timeless. What makes my carrot cake so special? It's extra moist, packed with nuts and raisins, and frosted generously with cream cheese frosting.

2 CUPS ALL-PURPOSE FLOUR

2 CUPS SUGAR

2 TEASPOONS BAKING POWDER

½ TEASPOON BAKING SODA

½ TEASPOON GROUND CINNAMON

½ TEASPOON SALT

4 EGGS, LIGHTLY BEATEN

3 CUPS FINELY SHREDDED CARROTS

¾ CUP VEGETABLE OIL

1 TABLESPOON GRATED ORANGE ZEST

1 CUP CHOPPED WALNUTS

1 CUP RAISINS

1 RECIPE CREAM CHEESE FROSTING (PAGE 142)

Preheat the oven to 350° F. Grease and flour two 9-inch round baking pans. Line the bottoms of the pans with parchment paper or wax paper. Grease the paper and set the pans aside.

In a large mixing bowl, combine the flour, sugar, baking powder, baking soda, cinnamon, and salt.

In another large mixing bowl, combine the eggs, carrots, oil, and orange zest. Add the egg mixture to the flour mixture and with a spoon, stir until combined. Stir in the walnuts and raisins and pour the batter into the prepared pans.

Bake for 30 to 35 minutes, or until a toothpick inserted in the center comes out clean. Cool the cake in the pans on a wire rack for 10 minutes. Remove from the pans and cool completely.

Place one cake layer on a serving platter and frost with Cream Cheese Frosting. Top with the remaining cake layer. Frost the top and sides with Cream Cheese Frosting.

SERVES 12

Cookies 'n' Cream Cake

This cake was the result of an accident compounded by an inspiration. Somehow, somebody tipped a whole box of Oreo cookies onto a freshly frosted buttercream layer. There was no way to get the Oreo crumbs out of the buttercream, so rather than throw it all out, we decided to make a crushed Oreo cookie layer cake. We wound up making a few of them, and when we brought them out, they sold immediately. Naturally, we added this "mistake" to our menu of cakes.

Chocolate Layer Cake

6 EGGS, SEPARATED, YOLKS AND WHITES RESERVED

1 TEASPOON VANILLA EXTRACT

1¼ CUPS SUGAR

½ CUP CAKE FLOUR

½ CUP UNSWEETENED COCOA POWDER

1 TEASPOON BAKING POWDER

6 TABLESPOONS (¾ STICK) UNSALTED BUTTER, MELTED

½ TEASPOON CREAM OF TARTAR

1 CUP BLACKOUT CREAM (PAGE 132)

1 CUP COARSELY CRUSHED CREME-FILLED CHOCOLATE SANDWICH
  COOKIES (ABOUT 10 COOKIES)

1 RECIPE BUTTERCREAM (PAGE 136)

12 WHOLE CREME-FILLED CHOCOLATE SANDWICH COOKIES,
  FOR DECORATING

Preheat the oven to 350° F. Grease and flour a 9-inch springform pan. Line the bottom of the pan with parchment paper or wax paper. Grease the paper and set aside.

In a mixing bowl, beat the egg yolks on high speed for about 5 minutes, or until thick and lemon colored. Add the vanilla. Reduce the speed to low and gradually beat in 1 cup of the sugar. Continue beating until the mixture thickens slightly and doubles in volume, about 5 minutes.

In a small bowl, combine the cake flour, cocoa, and baking powder. Sift ⅓ cup of the flour mixture over the egg yolk mixture and fold it in until combined. Repeat with ⅓-cup measures of the remaining flour mixture until it is all incorporated. Blend in the melted butter.

In a mixing bowl, beat the egg whites and cream of tartar on medium speed until soft peaks form, about 2 minutes. Gradually add the remaining ¼ cup of sugar to the egg whites, beating on high speed until stiff peaks form. Gently fold 1 cup of the beaten egg white mixture into the egg yolk mixture to lighten the batter, then fold the whole yolk mixture into the egg white mixture. Pour into the prepared pan.

Bake for 30 to 35 minutes, or until the cake springs back when lightly touched. Cool on a wire rack for 10 minutes. Remove from the pan and cool completely.

Using a long serrated knife, cut the cake in half horizontally, forming two equal layers. Place one layer on a serving plate. Frost the top with Blackout Cream and sprinkle with the crushed cookies. Top with the remaining cake layer. Frost the top and sides with the Buttercream, reserving ¾ cup of Buttercream for decorating the top of the cake. Fill a pastry bag with the remaining Buttercream. Using a large star tip, pipe 1 rosette in the center of the cake and 12 rosettes evenly spaced around the outer edges of the cake. Garnish the center and each rosette with a creme-filled chocolate sandwich cookie.

SERVES 12

French Nut Cake

We used to make this like everybody else, with ground nuts. But I wanted a nuttier flavor. I knew adding more nuts would throw off the texture of the cake. Then I came upon the idea of adding chopped nuts. Bingo! Chopped nuts give a much nuttier flavor that stands up beautifully to the garnishes of raspberry preserves, buttercream, and the final glaze of chocolate ganache.

3 OUNCES ALMOND PASTE

½ CUP (1 STICK) UNSALTED BUTTER, SOFTENED

½ CUP VEGETABLE SHORTENING

1 TEASPOON SALT

1¼ CUPS FIRMLY PACKED LIGHT BROWN SUGAR

5 EGGS

1 TABLESPOON VANILLA EXTRACT

2½ CUPS SPONGE CAKE CRUMBS (PAGE 153)

2 CUPS FINELY CHOPPED WALNUTS

2 TABLESPOONS SEEDLESS RASPBERRY PRESERVES

1 RECIPE BUTTERCREAM (PAGE 136)

1 RECIPE CHOCOLATE GANACHE (PAGE 145)

Preheat the oven to 350°F. Generously grease and flour a 9-inch springform pan. Line the bottom with parchment paper or wax paper. Grease the paper and set aside.

Using a grater or food processor, grate or shred the almond paste into a large mixing bowl.

On low speed, beat the almond paste, butter, shortening, salt, and brown sugar until light and fluffy. Gradually add the eggs, one at a time, beating well after each addition. Add the vanilla. Gradually add the cake crumbs and walnuts, occasionally scraping down the sides of the bowl. Beat for an additional 4 to 5 minutes.

Scrape the batter into the prepared pan and use the back of a spoon to spread evenly. Bake for 35 to 45 minutes, or until a toothpick inserted in the center comes out clean. Cool on a wire rack for 15 minutes. Remove from the pan and cool completely.

Using a long serrated knife, cut the cake in half horizontally, forming two equal layers. Spread the bottom layer with raspberry preserves and top with a thin layer of the Buttercream. Top with the remaining cake layer. Frost the top and sides with the remaining Buttercream. Refrigerate the cake for 1 hour, or until the Buttercream is firm. Remove the cake from the refrigerator and place on a wire rack over a baking sheet. Using a metal spatula, spread the Chocolate Ganache evenly over the top and sides of the cake. Refrigerate the cake for 10 to 15 minutes to set the ganache and chill at least 4 hours before cutting and serving.

SERVES 12

Chocolate Ganache Cake

We really should have called this cake the Chocolate Lover's Chocolate Chocolate Chocolate Chocolate Cake for the four forms of chocolate it contains—but all that wouldn't have fit on the sign on our display case! So we let the cake speak for itself: It's a chocolate cake filled with chocolate mousse, frosted with chocolate buttercream, and glazed with chocolate ganache. Remember to refrigerate the cake before pouring on the glaze. I like to serve each slice topped with billows of whipped cream.

Chocolate Layer Cake

6 EGGS, SEPARATED, YOLKS AND WHITES RESERVED

1 TEASPOON VANILLA EXTRACT

1¼ CUPS SUGAR

½ CUP CAKE FLOUR

½ CUP UNSWEETENED COCOA POWDER, PLUS ADDITIONAL FOR DUSTING

1 TEASPOON BAKING POWDER

6 TABLESPOONS (¾ STICK) UNSALTED BUTTER, MELTED

½ TEASPOON CREAM OF TARTAR

1 CUP CHOCOLATE MOUSSE (PAGE 133)

1 RECIPE CHOCOLATE BUTTERCREAM (PAGE 138)

1 RECIPE CHOCOLATE GANACHE (PAGE 145)

Preheat the oven to 350°F. Grease and flour a 9-inch springform pan. Line the bottom of the pan with parchment paper or wax paper. Grease the paper and set aside.

In a mixing bowl, beat the egg yolks on high speed for about 5 minutes, or until thick and lemon colored. Add the vanilla. Reduce the speed to low and gradually beat in 1 cup of the sugar. Continue beating until the mixture thickens slightly and doubles in volume, about 5 minutes.

In a small bowl, combine the cake flour, cocoa, and baking powder. Sift $1/3$ cup of the flour mixture over the egg yolk mixture and fold it in until combined. Repeat with $1/3$-cup measures of the remaining flour mixture until it is all incorporated. Blend in the melted butter.

In a mixing bowl, beat the egg whites and cream of tartar on medium speed until soft peaks form, about 2 minutes. Gradually add the remaining $1/4$ cup of sugar to the egg whites, beating on high speed until stiff peaks form. Gently fold 1 cup of the beaten egg white mixture into the egg yolk mixture to lighten the batter, then fold the whole yolk mixture into the egg white mixture. Pour into the prepared pan.

Bake for 30 to 35 minutes, or until the cake springs back when lightly touched. Cool on a wire rack for 10 minutes. Remove from the pan and cool completely.

Using a long serrated knife, cut the cake in half horizontally, forming 2 equal layers. Place one layer on a serving plate and spread with the Chocolate Mousse. Top with the remaining cake layer. Frost the top and sides with the Chocolate Buttercream. Refrigerate the cake for 1 hour. Place the cake on a wire rack set over a baking sheet. Using a metal spatula, spread the Chocolate Ganache evenly over the top and sides of the cake. Refrigerate for 10 to 15 minutes to set the ganache.

To serve, dust with additional cocoa powder.

SERVES 12

Pinwheel Cake

If it's true that we eat with our eyes before we eat with our mouths, then this cake succeeds on both levels. A white layer cake filled with chocolate mousse and topped with chocolate buttercream, it's decorated with chocolate sprinkles and triangles. If you need a cake for a party, it's a guaranteed conversation piece.

White Layer Cake

1 CUP SIFTED CAKE FLOUR

1 TEASPOON BAKING POWDER

¼ TEASPOON SALT

6 EGGS, SEPARATED, YOLKS AND WHITES RESERVED

¾ CUP PLUS 2 TABLESPOONS SUGAR

1 TEASPOON VANILLA EXTRACT

6 TABLESPOONS (¾ STICK) UNSALTED BUTTER, MELTED

½ TEASPOON CREAM OF TARTAR

6 OUNCES GOOD-QUALITY SEMISWEET CHOCOLATE

1 CUP CHOCOLATE MOUSSE (PAGE 133)

1 RECIPE CHOCOLATE BUTTERCREAM (PAGE 138)

½ CUP CHOCOLATE SPRINKLES

Preheat the oven to 350° F. Grease and flour a 9-inch springform pan. Line the bottom of the pan with parchment paper or wax paper. Grease the paper and set aside.

In a medium-size bowl, sift together the cake flour, baking powder, and salt. In another bowl, beat the egg yolks on high speed until thick and lemon colored, about 5 minutes. Reduce the speed to low and gradually beat in ¾ cup of sugar. Continue beating until the mixture thickens slightly and doubles in volume, about 5 minutes. Beat in the vanilla.

Sift ⅓ cup of the flour mixture over the egg yolk mixture and gently fold it in until combined. Repeat with ⅓-cup measures of the remaining flour mixture. Blend in the melted butter.

In a mixing bowl, beat the egg whites and cream of tartar on medium speed until soft peaks form. Gradually add the remaining 2 tablespoons sugar, beating on high speed until stiff peaks form. Gently fold the egg whites into the batter.

Spoon the batter into the prepared pan. Bake for 25 to 30 minutes, or until the center springs back when lightly touched. Cool on a wire rack for 10 minutes. Remove from the pan and cool completely.

To make the chocolate triangles, line a flat baking sheet with parchment paper and draw a 9-inch circle on the paper. In the top of a double boiler set over hot, not simmering, water, melt the chocolate and let it cool slightly. Pour the melted chocolate in the center of the traced circle and using a small metal spatula, spread the chocolate evenly until it fills the circle. Refrigerate the baking sheet for 5 to 10 minutes, until the chocolate feels firm but not brittle. With a long sharp knife, cut the circles into 12 wedges. Let harden completely.

Using a long serrated knife, cut the cake in half horizontally, forming two equal layers. Place one layer on a serving plate and frost with the Chocolate Mousse. Top with the remaining cake layer. Frost the top and sides with the Chocolate Buttercream, reserving ¾ cup. Decorate the sides of the cake with chocolate sprinkles.

Fill a pastry bag with the remaining ¾ cup Chocolate Buttercream. Using a large star tip, pipe 1 rosette in the top center of the cake and 12 rosettes evenly spaced around the top outer edge. Place 12 chocolate triangles around the top of the cake, placing each so that the widest portion rests at a slight angle on a piped rosette at the edge of the cake.

SERVES 12

Mocha Cake

A *couple of my customers are real coffee fanatics. If they're not drinking their morning coffee at Bruce's, they're home grinding their own beans and getting their brew just right. I keep them in mind when we bake this white layer cake with coffee buttercream drizzled with melted chocolate. For an extra kick, I top the cake with chocolate-covered coffee beans.*

White Layer Cake

1 CUP SIFTED CAKE FLOUR

1 TEASPOON BAKING POWDER

¼ TEASPOON SALT

6 EGGS SEPARATED, YOLKS AND WHITES RESERVED

¾ CUP PLUS 2 TABLESPOONS SUGAR

1 TEASPOON VANILLA EXTRACT

6 TABLESPOONS (¾ STICK) UNSALTED BUTTER, MELTED

½ TEASPOON CREAM OF TARTAR

1 RECIPE COFFEE BUTTERCREAM (PAGE 140)

½ CUP FINELY CHOPPED WALNUTS

13 CHOCOLATE-COVERED ESPRESSO BEANS

4 OUNCES GOOD-QUALITY SEMISWEET CHOCOLATE, MELTED AND COOLED

Preheat the oven to 350° F. Grease and flour a 9-inch springform pan. Line the bottom of the pan with parchment paper or wax paper. Grease the paper and set aside.

In a medium-size bowl, sift together the cake flour, baking powder, and salt.

In another mixing bowl, beat the egg yolks on high speed until thick and lemon colored, about 5 minutes. Reduce the speed to low and gradually beat in ¾ cup of sugar. Continue beating until the mixture thickens slightly and doubles in volume, about 5 minutes. Beat in the vanilla.

Sift ⅓ cup of the flour mixture over the egg yolk mixture and gently fold it in until combined. Repeat with ⅓-cup measures of the remaining flour mixture. Blend in the melted butter.

In a mixing bowl, beat the egg whites and cream of tartar on medium speed until soft peaks form. Gradually add the remaining 2 tablespoons sugar, beating on high speed until stiff peaks form. Gently fold the egg whites into the batter.

Spoon the batter into the prepared pan. Bake for 25 to 30 minutes, or until the center springs back when lightly touched. Cool on a wire rack for 10 minutes. Remove from the pan and cool completely.

Using a long serrated knife, cut the cake in half horizontally, forming 2 equal layers. Place one layer on a serving plate and frost with part of the Coffee Buttercream. Top with the remaining cake layer. Frost the top and sides with the remaining Coffee Buttercream, reserving ¾ cup for decorating the top of the cake. Garnish the sides of the cake with finely chopped walnuts.

Fill a pastry bag with the remaining ¾ cup Coffee Buttercream. Using a large star tip, pipe 1 rosette in the top center of the cake and 12 rosettes evenly spaced around the top edges of the cake. Garnish each rosette with a chocolate-covered espresso bean. Before serving, drizzle the cake with melted chocolate.

SERVES 12

Cookies
and Bars

Brownies

I guess I inherited my habit of tinkering with recipes from my dad, who did the same thing in his bakeries. I was looking for a way to jazz up our brownies and one day I got the idea to frost them with chocolate ganache. It's an unorthodox match, but I think Dad would have been proud of the result: a simple walnut brownie topped with one of the pastry world's most elegant frostings.

5 OUNCES GOOD-QUALITY UNSWEETENED CHOCOLATE,
   MELTED AND COOLED

3/4 CUP (1½ STICKS) UNSALTED BUTTER, SOFTENED

1¾ CUPS SUGAR

3 EGGS

1 TEASPOON VANILLA EXTRACT

1 CUP ALL-PURPOSE FLOUR

1 CUP CHOPPED WALNUTS

1 RECIPE CHOCOLATE GANACHE (PAGE 145)

Preheat the oven to 350° F. Grease a 13×9×2-inch pan.

In a large mixing bowl, combine the melted chocolate and butter and stir until smooth. Add the sugar and stir with a wooden spoon until well blended. Add the eggs and vanilla and mix well. Mix in the flour and nuts and stir. Pour the batter into the prepared pan.

Bake for 30 to 40 minutes, or until the edges appear to be set (the center should still be soft). Do not overbake. Cool completely in the pan on a wire rack. Frost with the Chocolate Ganache. Refrigerate for 10 to 15 minutes to set the ganache.

MAKES 24 BROWNIES

Candy Brownies

One of our customers came to us with a special request: Could we make a scrumptious chocolate treat that could be served from a buffet as finger food? Of course we could, and after a bit of experimentation, we came up with these dainty brownies, which have been a standard in our bakery case and on our catering menu ever since. Pass them around at a party and watch them disappear.

3 CUPS CONFECTIONERS' SUGAR

3/4 CUP ALL-PURPOSE FLOUR

4 OUNCES GOOD-QUALITY UNSWEETENED CHOCOLATE,
   MELTED AND COOLED

2 EGGS

1 TABLESPOON VANILLA EXTRACT

1/2 CUP (1 STICK) UNSALTED BUTTER, MELTED

1 CUP CHOPPED WALNUTS

Preheat the oven to 350°F. Line a 13×9×2-inch pan with aluminum foil. Lightly grease the foil and set aside.

In a large mixing bowl, combine the sugar, flour, and melted chocolate and beat until combined. Add the eggs and vanilla, and continue beating, scraping down the sides of the bowl, until the mixture is smooth. Gradually add the melted butter and walnuts and mix to combine. Pour into the prepared pan.

Bake for 20 to 25 minutes, or until the edges appear to be set (the center should still be soft). Do not overbake. Cool completely on a wire rack. Remove the brownies from the pan and remove the foil.

To serve, cut into squares.

MAKES 24 BROWNIES

Peanut Butter Brownie Delight

When I create a new recipe, the first thing I do is put different combinations of flavors in my head, which, after all these years in the business, houses a pretty good "test kitchen." I was racking my brain for a brownie recipe that would make an old favorite new, and one day, I woke up with this formula. I knew right away that peanut butter spread between two halves of a split chocolate brownie and then glazed with chocolate ganache would be a winner, and when we baked it, I was right.

3 CUPS CONFECTIONERS' SUGAR

¾ CUP ALL-PURPOSE FLOUR

4 OUNCES UNSWEETENED CHOCOLATE, MELTED AND COOLED

2 EGGS

1 TEASPOON VANILLA EXTRACT

½ CUP (1 STICK) UNSALTED BUTTER, MELTED

1 CUP CHOPPED WALNUTS

½ CUP CREAMY PEANUT BUTTER

1 CUP BUTTERCREAM (PAGE 136)

1 CUP CHOCOLATE GANACHE (PAGE 145)

Preheat the oven to 350° F. Line a 13×9×2-inch pan with aluminum foil. Lightly grease the foil and set aside.

In a large mixing bowl, combine the sugar, flour, and melted chocolate and beat on medium speed until smooth. Add the eggs and vanilla and mix well. Gradually add the butter and walnuts and stir to combine. Pour into the prepared pan.

Bake for 20 to 25 minutes, or until the edges appear to be set (the center should still be soft). Do not overbake. Let cool completely.

Holding the edges of the foil, remove the brownies from the pan onto a flat surface. Remove the foil and cut the brownies in half down the center. Spread one side of each half with the peanut butter and Buttercream, and sandwich the halves together so the toppings meet.

Place the large brownie sandwich on a wire rack set over a baking sheet. Using a metal spatula, spread the Chocolate Ganache evenly over the top and sides of the brownie. Refrigerate 10 to 15 minutes to set the ganache.

To serve, cut into squares.

MAKES ABOUT 12 BROWNIES

Rugelach

Before raspberry and chocolate became fashionable, there were cinnamon-nut rugelach. I started making these when I was ten years old and working in my father's bakery on weekends. My father was proud of his rugelach and insisted on using only butter and cream cheese in them, never shortening. When he told me I could try cutting them, I was thrilled. It looked easy enough. All you had to do was take the dough, cut it into strips with a wheel knife, and then roll each strip into a crescent. I wheeled away happily, and suddenly I was done, but there weren't enough strips in front of me. I had made them too wide. I was crushed—and my father was none too happy either. He told me to go home for the rest of the day, which was the worst punishment he could have given me. But he never stayed mad, and the next day I was back at the bakery, cutting dough for rugelach. They're easy to do at home, especially if you roll out the dough in a circle and cut it into wedges, and remember to spread the wet fillings first, before the cinnamon and crumbs.

Cream Cheese Pastry

1 CUP (2 STICKS) UNSALTED BUTTER, CHILLED

1 8-OUNCE PACKAGE CREAM CHEESE, CHILLED

2 TABLESPOONS SUGAR

2 CUPS ALL-PURPOSE FLOUR

2 EGG YOLKS

1 TEASPOON VANILLA EXTRACT

Filling

1/2 CUP SUGAR

1 TABLESPOON GROUND CINNAMON

3/4 CUP SEEDLESS RASPBERRY PRESERVES

3/4 CUP DRIED CURRANTS

3/4 CUP FINELY CHOPPED WALNUTS

In a medium-size mixing bowl, combine the butter, cream cheese, sugar, and flour. Using a pastry blender or your fingertips, combine well until the mixture resembles coarse meal.

In a separate bowl, combine the egg yolks and vanilla. Add the yolks to the flour mixture and mix until smooth. Form the dough into three equal pieces. Form each piece into a round ball and on a clean work surface, with the palm of your hand, flatten the balls slightly and wrap each individually in plastic wrap. Refrigerate 5 or 6 hours or overnight.

Preheat the oven to 350° F. Line 2 baking sheets with parchment paper.

In a small bowl, combine the sugar and cinnamon and set aside.

On a floured board or pastry cloth, roll one piece of the chilled dough into a 12-inch circle about ¼ inch thick. Brush with ¼ cup raspberry preserves. Sprinkle with one third each of the cinnamon sugar, currants, and walnuts. With a long sharp knife, cut the circle into 16 wedges. Starting at the wide end, roll up each wedge jelly roll style. Place each piece, seam-side down, on the prepared baking sheets, leaving about 1 inch between each piece. Repeat with the remaining dough and filling ingredients.

Bake for 18 to 22 minutes, or until lightly browned. Let cool completely on a wire rack.

MAKES 48 COOKIES

Chocolate Rugelach

Remember the old advertising slogan for Levy's rye bread? Well, I've appropriated it for these treats: You don't have to be Jewish to love rugelach. These Old World-style cream cheese pastries are now beloved by everybody, as I've learned from standing behind the bakery counter. At Bruce's, the rugelach is made with pure butter and cream cheese, never shortening. The chocolate chips and chocolate smear that run through the center give them a decidedly New World update.

Cream Cheese Pastry

1 CUP (2 STICKS) UNSALTED BUTTER, CHILLED

1 8-OUNCE PACKAGE CREAM CHEESE, CHILLED

2 TABLESPOONS SUGAR

2 CUPS ALL-PURPOSE FLOUR

2 EGG YOLKS

1 TEASPOON VANILLA EXTRACT

Chocolate Filling

½ CUP SUGAR

1 TABLESPOON GROUND CINNAMON

8 OUNCES GOOD-QUALITY SEMISWEET CHOCOLATE,
   MELTED AND COOLED

¾ CUP MINI SEMISWEET CHOCOLATE CHIPS

In a medium-size mixing bowl, combine the butter, cream cheese, sugar, and flour. Using a pastry blender or your fingertips, combine well until the mixture resembles coarse meal.

In a separate bowl, combine the egg yolks and vanilla. Add the egg yolk mixture to the flour mixture and mix until smooth. Form the dough into three equal pieces. Form each piece into a round ball, flatten slightly with the palm of your hand, and wrap each piece individually in plastic. Refrigerate for 5 or 6 hours or overnight.

Preheat the oven to 350°F. Line 2 baking sheets with parchment paper.

In a small bowl, combine the sugar and cinnamon and set aside.

On a floured board or pastry cloth, roll one of the chilled dough balls into a 12-inch circle. Brush on one third of the melted chocolate and sprinkle with one third of the sugar-cinnamon mixture and one third of the mini chocolate chips. With a long sharp knife, cut the circle into 16 wedges. Starting at the wide end, roll up each wedge jelly roll style. Place each piece, seam-side down, on the parchment-lined baking sheets, leaving about 1 inch between each piece. Repeat with the remaining dough and filling ingredients.

Bake for 18 to 22 minutes, or until lightly browned. Let cool completely on a wire rack.

MAKES 48 COOKIES

Bruce's Chocolate Chip Cookies

In the 1980s, the chocolate chip cookie became a designer item, and the chocolate chip cookie market became very competitive. Of course, I couldn't resist trying to come up with my own version, and this is it. I took a ten-pound bar of imported dark chocolate and banged on it with a hammer. The result was a mountain of marvelous, odd-sized chocolate chunks. I poured them into the batter, along with a generous helping of walnuts, and Bruce's Chocolate Chip Cookie was born. At home, you no doubt won't be working with ten pounds of chocolate, and it's probably not a good idea to use a hammer on the kitchen counter, but the recipe below will produce the same rich cookie, bursting with chocolate and nuts.

1¾ CUPS FIRMLY PACKED LIGHT BROWN SUGAR

3 CUPS ALL-PURPOSE FLOUR

½ TEASPOON SALT

3 EGGS

2 TEASPOONS VANILLA EXTRACT

¾ CUP (1½ STICKS) UNSALTED BUTTER

2 CUPS COARSELY CHOPPED WALNUTS

1¼ POUNDS GOOD-QUALITY SEMISWEET CHOCOLATE, COARSELY CHOPPED

Preheat the oven to 350° F.

In a large mixing bowl, combine the brown sugar, flour, and salt. Beating at low speed, add the eggs, mixing well. Add the vanilla and mix until combined.

In a small saucepan over medium-high heat, bring the butter to a boil. Remove from the heat. Carefully add the butter to the flour mixture, mixing to combine. Stir in the walnuts and chocolate.

Using floured hands (the dough will be sticky), place generous tablespoonfuls of dough onto ungreased baking sheets.

Bake for 9 to 11 minutes, until golden brown. Remove to a wire rack and cool completely.

MAKES 42 COOKIES

Double Chocolate Chip Cookies with Macadamia Nuts

*M*y *partner Joel's daughters, Bonnie, Traci, and Keri, are crazy about these cookies, with their generous allotments of white and dark chocolate and macadamia nuts, and so is Joel. In fact, so is everybody who tries them. There's nothing like a homemade chocolate chip cookie and a glass of cold milk.*

1 CUP ALL-PURPOSE FLOUR

½ TEASPOON BAKING SODA

½ TEASPOON SALT

½ CUP (1 STICK) UNSALTED BUTTER, SOFTENED

½ CUP FIRMLY PACKED LIGHT BROWN SUGAR

¼ CUP SUGAR

1 EGG

1 TEASPOON VANILLA EXTRACT

¾ CUP COARSELY CHOPPED MACADAMIA NUTS

6 OUNCES GOOD-QUALITY BITTERSWEET CHOCOLATE, COARSELY CHOPPED

6 OUNCES WHITE CHOCOLATE, COARSELY CHOPPED

Preheat the oven to 375° F.

In a medium-size bowl, sift together the flour, baking soda, and salt and stir to combine with a wire whisk.

In a large mixing bowl, beat the butter on medium speed for 30 seconds, or until creamy. Add both sugars and continue beating for 2 to 3 minutes, until the mixture is light in texture and in color. Scrape down the sides of the bowl with a rubber spatula. Add the egg and vanilla and beat well.

On low speed, beat in the flour mixture in two additions, scraping down the sides of the bowl with a rubber spatula after each addition. Using a wooden spoon, stir in the macadamia nuts and chopped chocolate.

Shape the dough into balls and place on ungreased baking sheets 2 inches apart. Bake for 8 to 10 minutes, or until the edges are lightly browned.

Cool on the baking sheets for 2 minutes, then transfer to a wire rack to cool completely.

MAKES ABOUT 36 COOKIES

Continental Cookies

Fred Astaire and Ginger Rogers made the Continental a popular dance craze, and when my father Harry developed these walnut meringue cookies topped with chocolate buttercream rosettes and glazed with melted chocolate, he named them after the dance.

½ CUP SUGAR

2 TABLESPOONS (¼ STICK) UNSALTED BUTTER, SOFTENED

6 TABLESPOONS VEGETABLE SHORTENING

¾ CUP ALL-PURPOSE FLOUR

1 CUP FINELY GROUND WALNUTS

2 EGG WHITES

2 TEASPOONS VANILLA EXTRACT

1 CUP CHOCOLATE BUTTERCREAM (PAGE 138)

4 OUNCES GOOD-QUALITY SEMISWEET CHOCOLATE,
   MELTED AND COOLED

Preheat the oven to 350° F. Line 2 baking sheets with parchment paper.

In a large mixing bowl, cream together the sugar, butter, and shortening until light and fluffy. Add the flour and walnuts and stir to combine. Beat in the egg whites and vanilla.

Spoon the batter into a pastry bag fitted with a large round tip (½-inch opening). Pipe small circles with a diameter of 1 inch onto the prepared baking sheets. Bake for 9 to 11 minutes, or until the edges are lightly browned. Cool on a wire rack for 10 minutes. Remove from the baking sheets and cool completely.

Using a pastry bag with a large star tip, pipe a Chocolate Butter-cream rosette on each cookie. Refrigerate until the buttercream is hardened, about 15 minutes.

Place the cookies on a wire rack set over a baking sheet. Drizzle the melted chocolate over the cookies to cover. Let sit until the chocolate hardens, about 1 hour.

MAKES ABOUT 54 COOKIES

Chocolate-Filled Icebox Cookies

I was born a bit too late to remember the icemen making their rounds in Brooklyn, but I do remember my father telling me about them, and how they'd heft big blocks of ice with their special tongs and deposit them in the iceboxes that people had in the era before refrigeration. These cookies were called icebox cookies because that was where you would chill the rolled-up dough to make it easier to handle. You can also freeze the dough, well wrapped, for up to 3 months. When you're ready to bake, let it soften just enough so that it's easy to slice.

1½ CUPS ALL-PURPOSE FLOUR

¼ TEASPOON BAKING POWDER

¼ TEASPOON SALT

1 CUP CONFECTIONERS' SUGAR

½ CUP (1 STICK) UNSALTED BUTTER, SOFTENED

1 EGG

1 TEASPOON VANILLA EXTRACT

6 OUNCES GOOD-QUALITY SEMISWEET CHOCOLATE,
   MELTED AND COOLED

Preheat the oven to 350° F.

In a small bowl, stir together the flour, baking powder, and salt; set aside.

In a large mixing bowl, cream together the sugar and butter until light and fluffy. Beat in the egg and vanilla. Add the flour mixture to the batter and continue beating until well combined. On a clean work surface, divide the dough in half and shape each half into a log about 5 inches long with a diameter of 1½ inches. Wrap the logs separately in plastic and chill 30 minutes, or until firm.

Remove the plastic wrap and cut the logs into ¼-inch slices. Place the cookies on ungreased baking sheets. With your thumb, gently press down to make an indentation in the center of each cookie. Bake for 8 to 10 minutes, or until slightly golden around the edges. Cool on a wire rack for 2 minutes. Remove from the baking sheets and cool completely.

Spoon the chocolate into a pastry bag fitted with a large plain round tip (½-inch opening). Pipe a small amount of chocolate into the center of each cookie. Let the chocolate harden for 1 hour before serving.

RASPBERRY-FILLED ICEBOX COOKIES: Substitute ¼ cup seedless raspberry preserves for the chocolate. Prepare the recipe as directed. Using a small spoon, fill each cookie center with ¼ teaspoon raspberry preserves. Serve immediately.

MAKES ABOUT 48 TO 60 COOKIES

French Butter Cookies

¶ *I love everything we sell at Bruce's but these heavenly little butter cookie sandwiches are a personal favorite. Often, I fill them with raspberry preserves, but when the mood strikes, I use apricot instead. Add a litte chocolate ganache and it's ooh la la! They're great alone or with a dish of ice cream.*

1 CUP (2 STICKS) UNSALTED BUTTER, SOFTENED

⅔ CUP SUGAR

3 EGG YOLKS

1 TEASPOON VANILLA EXTRACT

2½ CUPS ALL-PURPOSE FLOUR

½ TEASPOON SALT

1 RECIPE CHOCOLATE GANACHE (PAGE 145)

½ CUP SEEDLESS RASPBERRY PRESERVES

Preheat the oven to 375° F. Grease 2 baking sheets.

In a large mixing bowl, cream together the butter and sugar at medium speed until light and fluffy. Add the egg yolks, one at a time, beating well after each addition. Mix in the vanilla.

Add the flour and salt to the butter mixture and beat at low speed until well combined.

Spoon the dough into a pastry bag fitted with a large fluted tip. Pipe the dough onto the prepared baking sheets in 1½-inch-diameter circles, leaving about 2 inches between each cookie.

Bake for 8 to 9 minutes, until very light golden brown. Cool on a wire rack for 5 minutes. Remove from the baking sheets and cool completely.

To assemble, spread the Chocolate Ganache on the bottom of half of the cookies and raspberry preserves on the bottom of the remaining cookies. Press the toppings together to make a sandwich. If desired, drizzle or dip the cookies in the Chocolate Ganache. Let the chocolate set at room temperature for 2 hours.

MAKES ABOUT 24 COOKIES

Coconut Macaroons

We bake thousands upon thousands of pounds of macaroons for Passover and almost as many for Rosh Hashanah and Yom Kippur. You'd think after all that I wouldn't want to look at another macaroon, but when I finally leave the shop for my own family celebration, I still look forward to enjoying these traditional sweets. You can serve them plain or dress them up by dipping them in chocolate or raspberry or strawberry sauce. Note that if you want the macaroons to be kosher for Passover, you must use matzo cake meal instead of flour.

1½ CUPS SWEETENED FLAKED COCONUT

⅓ CUP SUGAR

3 TABLESPOONS ALL-PURPOSE FLOUR OR MATZO CAKE MEAL

¼ TEASPOON SALT

2 EGG WHITES

½ TEASPOON ALMOND EXTRACT

Preheat the oven to 325° F. Lightly grease a baking sheet.

In a large bowl, combine the coconut, sugar, flour, and salt. Mix in the egg whites and almond extract and stir until thoroughly combined.

Drop from tablespoons onto the prepared baking sheet. Bake for 20 to 25 minutes, or until the edges are golden brown. Remove from the baking sheet immediately and cool completely on a wire rack.

MAKES 12 TO 18 COOKIES

Homemade Sugar Cookies

*M*ost times, granulated sugar goes into the cookie batter and confectioners' sugar is dusted on the outside when the cookies are done. In this case, it's just the opposite. The result: a finer-textured sugar cookie that's light and delicious.

1½ CUPS CONFECTIONERS' SUGAR, SIFTED

1 CUP (2 STICKS) UNSALTED BUTTER, SOFTENED

1 EGG

2 TEASPOONS ALMOND EXTRACT

2½ CUPS ALL-PURPOSE FLOUR

1 TEASPOON BAKING SODA

1 TEASPOON CREAM OF TARTAR

1 CUP GRANULATED SUGAR

Preheat the oven to 375°F.

In a large mixing bowl on medium speed, beat together the confectioners' sugar and butter until light and fluffy. Add the egg and almond extract and beat well. In a small bowl, stir together the flour, baking soda, and cream of tartar and gradually add to the creamed mixture. Divide the dough in half and form each half into a ball. Flatten the balls of dough into disk shapes and wrap separately in plastic wrap. Refrigerate for 1 hour, until chilled.

On a well-floured surface, roll out half of the dough at a time to ¼-inch thickness. Using a cookie cutter, cut into shapes and sprinkle with granulated sugar. Bake on ungreased baking sheets for 5 to 8 minutes, or until lightly browned at the edges. Remove from the oven and sprinkle with additional sugar. Cool on the baking sheets for 2 minutes, then remove to a wire rack and cool completely.

MAKES ABOUT 36 COOKIES

Jewish Biscotti

*W*hen *I first tasted biscotti, I realized it had a lot in common with mandelbrot, and I wondered what would happen if I sliced and toasted some Bruce's Bakery mandelbrot. I wish all my ideas were this good!*

Mandelbrot

4 OUNCES ALMOND PASTE

1 CUP SUGAR

$2/3$ CUP VEGETABLE SHORTENING

3 OUNCES FARMER CHEESE

2 EGGS

2 EGG YOLKS

2 TEASPOONS VANILLA EXTRACT

2 TEASPOONS ALMOND EXTRACT

$3\frac{1}{2}$ CUPS ALL-PURPOSE FLOUR

1 TEASPOON BAKING POWDER

$\frac{1}{2}$ TEASPOON BAKING SODA

$\frac{1}{2}$ TEASPOON SALT

$\frac{1}{4}$ CUP MILK

2 CUPS SEMISWEET CHOCOLATE CHIPS

3 OUNCES SEMISWEET CHOCOLATE, MELTED AND COOLED

Topping

2 TABLESPOONS FINELY CHOPPED WALNUTS

$1\frac{1}{2}$ TABLESPOONS SUGAR

$\frac{1}{4}$ TEASPOON GROUND CINNAMON

1 EGG, LIGHTLY BEATEN

Biscotti Topping

¼ CUP (½ STICK) UNSALTED BUTTER, MELTED

2 TABLESPOONS SUGAR

¾ TEASPOON GROUND CINNAMON

Preheat the oven to 350° F. Line a baking sheet with parchment paper.

Using a grater or food processor, grate or shred the almond paste into a large mixing bowl. Add the sugar and mix well on low speed. Add the shortening and farmer cheese and continue beating until smooth. Add the eggs and egg yolks, one at a time, mixing well after each addition, then add the vanilla and almond extracts and beat until blended.

In a separate bowl, combine the flour, baking powder, baking soda, and salt. Gradually add the flour mixture to the batter, alternating with the milk, until well combined. Stir in the chocolate chips. Place the dough on a lightly floured cutting board and drizzle with the melted chocolate. Using floured hands (the dough will be sticky), knead the dough, incorporating the drizzled chocolate and creating a marbleized effect. In a small bowl, combine the chopped nuts, sugar, and cinnamon.

Divide the dough into three equal pieces. Form each piece into an oval football shape about 6 inches long. Place on the prepared baking sheet and brush with the beaten egg. Sprinkle each loaf with the topping mixture.

Bake 45 to 55 minutes, until the dough is richly golden and seems dry to the touch. Remove from the oven and cool completely on a wire rack.

Transfer the pastry to a cutting board. Using a long serrated knife, cut the pastry on the diagonal into slices about ¾ inch thick. Using a

continued on next page

wide metal spatula, transfer the cut cookies to an ungreased baking sheet. Brush with the melted butter.

In a small bowl, combine the sugar and cinnamon and sprinkle it over the cookies. Bake at 300° F. for 10 minutes, or until lightly browned.

Turn the cookies over and bake an additional 10 to 15 minutes, or until the cookies are golden brown and firm to the touch. Immediately remove from the baking sheet and cool completely on a wire rack.

MAKES ABOUT 30 BISCOTTI

Leaf Cookies

*T*hese cookies are delicious on their own, but at Bruce's we often use them to decorate cakes. We write on the leaves in frosting and then press them into the cake. Decorating with leaf cookies has become a popular option on our special-occasion cake menu. And you don't have to be an artist to create them: Four-inch leaf stencils give these old-fashioned, buttery cookies their shape. You can find the stencils at most kitchen supply stores.

¼ CUP (½ STICK) UNSALTED BUTTER, SOFTENED

⅓ CUP SUGAR

1 EGG

¼ TEASPOON VANILLA EXTRACT

¾ CUP PLUS 2 TABLESPOONS SIFTED CAKE FLOUR

6 TABLESPOONS FINELY GROUND WALNUTS

6 OUNCES GOOD-QUALITY SEMISWEET CHOCOLATE, MELTED AND COOLED

Preheat the oven to 350° F. Grease and lightly flour 2 baking sheets.

In a large mixing bowl, cream together the butter and sugar until light and fluffy. Add the egg and the vanilla. Add the flour and walnuts and mix well.

Place the leaf stencil onto a prepared baking sheet. Press the mixture through the stencil with a spatula. Repeat the process so that there are 6 cookies on each baking sheet.

Bake for 8 to 10 minutes, or until the edges are golden brown. Remove the cookies immediately from the baking sheet and cool on a wire rack.

Dip or spread melted chocolate on the bottoms of each cookie. Let the chocolate set at room temperature several hours or overnight.

MAKES ABOUT 12 COOKIES

Lace Cookies

Customers sometimes ask me how come my lace cookies look so, well, lacy. Here is the answer: The trick to making perfect lace cookies is to chop the walnuts fine. This will create the "holes" that give the cookies their lacy appearance. These delicate cookies expand significantly while they bake, so allow at least 3 inches between them when you place them on the baking sheets.

6 TABLESPOONS (3/4 STICK) UNSALTED BUTTER

1/4 CUP SUGAR

2 TABLESPOONS LIGHT CORN SYRUP

1 CUP FINELY CHOPPED WALNUTS

1/4 CUP ALL-PURPOSE FLOUR

1/8 TEASPOON SALT

1/8 TEASPOON GROUND CINNAMON

8 OUNCES GOOD-QUALITY SEMISWEET CHOCOLATE,
    MELTED AND COOLED

Preheat the oven to 350° F. Grease and lightly flour a baking sheet.

In a medium-size saucepan over medium-high heat, combine the butter, 1/3 cup water, the sugar, and corn syrup. Bring to a full rolling boil, stirring occasionally. Remove from the heat and stir in the walnuts, flour, salt, and cinnamon.

Using a pastry bag without a tip, pipe the dough into small circles with a diameter of 1/2 inch onto the prepared baking sheet, leaving about 3 inches of space between each cookie.

Bake for 8 to 10 minutes, or until the edges are lightly browned. Cool on the baking sheet 1 minute, then carefully transfer the cookies to wax paper and cool completely.

Repeat with the remaining batter, greasing and flouring the baking sheet between batches.

To decorate the cookies, spread the bottom of each cookie with the melted chocolate. Sandwich 2 cookies together and then dip them halfway into the melted chocolate. Let rest on wax paper until the chocolate sets, about 1 hour.

MAKES ABOUT 18 COOKIES

Old-Fashioned Lemon Bars

*T*hese luscious bars are full of tart citrusy flavor, the kind that makes you pucker up with pleasure. Serve them at tea time or as a dessert paired with fresh berries. I learned from my father that the thinner-skinned, sweeter lemons, such as Meyer lemons, are the juiciest. The best way to extract the most juice is to have the lemons at room temperature and then roll them around on the counter with the flat of your hand.

Crust

1 CUP ALL-PURPOSE FLOUR

½ CUP (1 STICK) UNSALTED BUTTER, SOFTENED

¼ CUP CONFECTIONERS' SUGAR

1 TABLESPOON GRATED LEMON ZEST

Lemon Filling

¾ CUP SUGAR

2 EGGS

⅓ CUP FRESH LEMON JUICE

1 TABLESPOON GRATED LEMON ZEST

2 TABLESPOONS ALL-PURPOSE FLOUR

½ TEASPOON BAKING POWDER

CONFECTIONERS' SUGAR, FOR DUSTING

Preheat the oven to 350° F.

To prepare the crust, in a medium-size mixing bowl, combine the flour, butter, confectioners' sugar, and lemon zest. Beat on low speed until combined. Press the mixture into an ungreased 8-inch square baking pan, building up ½-inch edges. Bake the crust until light golden brown, about 20 minutes.

To prepare the filling, in a large mixing bowl, beat together the sugar, eggs, lemon juice, and lemon zest. In a small bowl, combine the flour and baking powder; stir into the egg mixture. Pour the filling over the baked crust.

Bake for 25 minutes, or until lightly browned around the edges and the center appears set. Cool in the pan on a wire rack.

Dust with sifted confectioners' sugar, cut into 16 bars, and serve.

MAKES 16 BARS

Chocolate-Dipped Shortbread

Few things are better with a cup of coffee or tea than shortbread—especially a shortbread jam-packed with sweet butter and dipped in smooth bittersweet chocolate. These delectable little rectangles are so buttery that the dough is tricky to roll out. For best results, roll only a small portion of dough at a time, leaving the rest refrigerated until ready to use.

⅔ CUP CONFECTIONERS' SUGAR, SIFTED

1 CUP (2 STICKS) UNSALTED BUTTER, SOFTENED

1 TEASPOON VANILLA EXTRACT

2 CUPS ALL-PURPOSE FLOUR

½ TEASPOON SALT

12 OUNCES GOOD-QUALITY BITTERSWEET CHOCOLATE, MELTED

In a large mixing bowl, combine the confectioners' sugar and butter and beat until light and fluffy. Add the vanilla and combine well. In a small bowl, sift together the flour and salt. Add to the sugar mixture and beat until well combined.

Divide the dough in half and flatten each half into a rectangle about 4 × 6 inches. Wrap each piece in plastic and refrigerate for 1 hour, or until firm enough to roll.

Position one rack in the top third of the oven and another in the bottom third and preheat to 325° F.

Lightly dust 1 piece of the dough with flour. Place the dough between 2 sheets of parchment or wax paper. Using a rolling pin, roll out the dough to a rectangle slightly larger than 6 × 12 inches. Remove the top piece of paper. Using a ruler and a sharp knife, trim the edges to make an even 6 × 12-inch rectangle. Cut the rectangle lengthwise into six 1-inch-wide strips. Then cut each strip into six 2-inch pieces, to form a total of 36 cookies.

Using a metal spatula, carefully transfer the cut cookies to an ungreased baking sheet, leaving about 1 inch of space between the cookies. Gather any scraps of dough together into a ball and flatten into a rectangle. Wrap the dough in plastic wrap and refrigerate until firm.

Bake the cookies for 12 to 15 minutes, or until they are golden brown on the bottom. Cool the cookies on the baking sheets on wire racks for 1 to 2 minutes. Using a metal spatula, transfer the cookies to a wire rack to cool completely. Repeat the process with the remaining chilled dough.

Line 2 baking sheets with wax paper. Dip 1 shortbread cookie into the melted chocolate, completely coating the bottom third of the cookie. Shake off any excess chocolate and place on the prepared baking sheet. Repeat with the remaining cookies, rewarming the melted chocolate if necessary. Let the cookies sit at room temperature about 1 hour, or until the chocolate is set.

MAKES 5 TO 6 DOZEN COOKIES

Pies
and
Tarts

Apple Pie

Baking is an art, a science, and an act of love. An art, because it must please the eye. A science, because it depends on chemical reactions between precisely measured ingredients (as anyone who's ever added a little too much baking powder to the batter mix knows only too well!). Baking is an act of love because you do it to nourish and delight those around you, whether in a commercial bakery or your kitchen at home. And what says love better than an apple pie? I like to use a combination of Granny Smith and Golden Delicious for a sweet-tart flavor. Serve it warm and top it off with big scoops of vanilla ice cream.

1 RECIPE PASTRY FOR DOUBLE-CRUST PIE (PAGE 155)

Filling

6 CUPS THINLY SLICED PEELED COOKING APPLES
(ABOUT 6 LARGE APPLES OR 2½ POUNDS)

1 TABLESPOON LEMON JUICE

¾ CUP SUGAR

2 TABLESPOONS ALL-PURPOSE FLOUR

½ TEASPOON GROUND CINNAMON

2 TABLESPOONS (¼ STICK) UNSALTED BUTTER,
CUT INTO SMALL PIECES

1 EGG, LIGHTLY BEATEN

Prepare the pastry according to the directions on page 155. Divide the dough in half and form each half into a ball. Roll out 1 ball of dough according to the directions. Line a 9-inch pie plate with the pastry and set aside.

Preheat the oven to 375° F.

In a large mixing bowl, combine the apples, lemon juice, sugar, flour, and cinnamon and toss well.

Spoon the apple mixture into the pie plate and dot the top with the pieces of butter. Trim any overhanging pastry to the edge of the pie plate. Roll the remaining dough into a 10-inch circle that will be the top crust of the pie. Top the pie with the remaining crust, allowing a 1-inch overlap of top pastry around the edge. Fold the edge of the top crust under the bottom crust. Press well to seal and form a stand-up rim of pastry to flute. Flute the edge as desired. Cut about eight 1-inch slits in the top pastry to allow the steam to escape.

Brush the top of the crust with the beaten egg. Cover the edge of the pie with a 2-inch strip of aluminum foil to prevent excessive browning. Bake for 25 minutes, then remove the foil and bake for an additional 25 to 30 minutes, or until the top is golden brown. Cool completely on a wire rack.

SERVES 8

Fresh Blueberry Tart

A little old European baker who worked for my father used to say, *"If something is good, you don't mind waiting for it."* That's the way it is with fresh blueberries. They're so good, you don't mind waiting all year for them. This tart is chock full of fresh berries and delivers a robust *"berry"* flavor in every bite. It's a nice change from the usual two-crust berry pie.

1 RECIPE BAKED TART CRUST (PAGE 154)

5 CUPS FRESH BLUEBERRIES

1 CUP SUGAR

3 TABLESPOONS CORNSTARCH

CONFECTIONERS' SUGAR, FOR DUSTING

Prepare the Baked Tart Crust in a 9-inch tart pan with a removable bottom.

In a small bowl, using the back of a spoon, mash enough blueberries to measure 1 cup. In a 2-quart saucepan, mix together the sugar and cornstarch. Gradually stir in ½ cup water and the mashed blueberries. Cook over medium heat, stirring constantly, until the mixture thickens and boils, about 5 minutes. Boil and stir for 1 minute, then remove from the heat and cool.

Set 1 cup of blueberries aside for the top of the tart. Fill the tart shell with the blueberries and top with the cooked blueberry mixture. Top with the remaining fresh blueberries. Refrigerate until set, at least 3 hours.

To serve, dust with sifted confectioners' sugar.

SERVES 8

Triple Berry Tart

Summer fruits and berries are my absolute favorite, both to look at and to eat, so I designed this tart to feature as many berries as I could. The cookie-like dough filled with creamy custard and crowned with fresh berries positively bursts with the colors and flavors of summer.

1 RECIPE BAKED TART CRUST (PAGE 154)

1 RECIPE CUSTARD FILLING (PAGE 144)

1 RECIPE SPONGE CAKE (PAGE 152)

3 TABLESPOONS SEEDLESS RASPBERRY PRESERVES

STRAWBERRIES, BLUEBERRIES, AND RASPBERRIES, FOR GARNISH

CONFECTIONERS' SUGAR, FOR DUSTING

Prepare the Baked Tart Crust in a 9-inch tart pan with a removable bottom.

Fill the baked tart shell with the custard. Slice the sponge cake in half horizontally. Place one layer on top of the custard; set the remaining layer aside for another use. Spread the raspberry preserves on top of the sponge cake layer.

Garnish with the fruit and dust with the sifted confectioners' sugar. Chill 2 hours before serving.

SERVES 8

Cherry Almond Tart

You can use either sweet or sour cherries in this recipe. At the bakery we often use a combination of both. The deep red cherries you find in the supermarket are sweet cherries; small, light-colored sour cherries, such as Montmorency, are often found at farmer's markets. If you don't have a cherry pitter, use a chopstick to push the pits straight through.

Pastry

1¾ CUPS ALL-PURPOSE FLOUR

2 TABLESPOONS FINELY GROUND ALMONDS

1 TABLESPOON SUGAR

11 TABLESPOONS (⅞ STICK) UNSALTED BUTTER,
   CHILLED AND CUT INTO ½-INCH PIECES

4 TO 5 TABLESPOONS ICE WATER

Cherry Almond Filling

½ CUP (1 STICK) UNSALTED BUTTER, SOFTENED

½ CUP SUGAR

1 EGG

1 CUP FINELY GROUND ALMONDS

1 TABLESPOON CHERRY-FLAVORED LIQUEUR

1 TEASPOON ALMOND EXTRACT

1 TABLESPOON ALL-PURPOSE FLOUR

1 POUND FRESH SWEET OR SOUR CHERRIES, PITTED

CONFECTIONERS' SUGAR, FOR DUSTING

To prepare the pastry, in the bowl of a food processor, blend together the flour, ground almonds, and sugar. Add the butter and process, pulsing the machine on and off until the mixture resembles coarse meal. Sprinkle in 4 tablespoons of the ice water and process until moist clumps form. If the dough is still dry, add the remaining water 1 teaspoon at a time. Shape the dough into a ball.

On a lightly floured surface using a floured rolling pin, roll out the dough into a 12-inch circle about 1/8 inch thick. Transfer to a 10-inch tart pan with a removable bottom. Press the dough gently into place, then trim the excess dough from around the edges. Refrigerate the tart shell for 20 to 30 minutes, or until firm.

Preheat the oven to 425°F.

To prepare the filling, in a large mixing bowl, cream together the butter and the sugar until light and fluffy. Add the egg, ground almonds, liqueur, almond extract, and flour, and beat until smooth. Spread the mixture evenly in the chilled tart shell. Arrange the cherries in a single layer on top of the filling in the pastry shell.

Bake the tart for 50 to 60 minutes, or until the tart shell is golden and the filling has puffed and is golden brown. Remove from the oven and cool on a wire rack.

Dust with sifted confectioners' sugar and serve.

SERVES 10

Honey-Nut Tartlets

My father developed these scrumptious tarts. The secret is boiling the honey with the nuts. Clover honey, with its light, delicate flavor, works well with walnuts, which should be chopped by hand; a food processor will give you walnut paste instead of chopped nuts. You can also make cookies from this recipe: Roll the dough out on a cookie sheet and top it with the honey-nut mixture. When it's baked and cooled, cut it into bar cookies and dip them into melted semisweet chocolate.

Pastry

2 CUPS ALL-PURPOSE FLOUR

½ TEASPOON SALT

⅔ CUP VEGETABLE SHORTENING, CHILLED

6 TO 7 TABLESPOONS ICE WATER

Honey-Nut Filling

1 CUP HONEY, PREFERABLY CLOVER HONEY

1 CUP SUGAR

1 CUP (2 STICKS) UNSALTED BUTTER

1 TEASPOON GROUND CINNAMON

5 CUPS WALNUTS, COARSELY CHOPPED

Preheat the oven to 375°F. Grease ten 4- to 4½-inch tart pans with removable bottoms and set aside.

To prepare the pastry, in a medium-size mixing bowl, stir together the flour and salt. Using a pastry blender, or two knives, cut in the shortening until the mixture is crumbled into pea-size pieces. Sprinkle in the water, 1 tablespoon at a time, and mix with a fork until all the flour is moistened and the dough almost cleans the side of the bowl, adding more water if necessary. Shape the dough into two balls.

On a lightly floured surface, use the palm of your hand to flatten one of the balls of dough. Working from the center out, roll the dough into a large circle about 12 inches in diameter. Using a sharp knife, cut into small circles to fit the tartlet pans. Repeat with the remaining dough, combining the scraps and rerolling if necessary. Press the pastry into the bottom and up the sides of each tart pan and line the shells with a double thickness of foil.

Bake for 8 minutes, then remove the foil and bake an additional 3 to 4 more minutes, until the crust is dry and set. Cool completely. Reduce the oven temperature to 350° F.

In a large saucepan over medium heat, combine the honey, sugar, butter, and cinnamon. Bring to a boil, then stir in the walnuts. Remove from the heat. Fill the tartlet pans with the honey-walnut mixture and bake on a baking sheet for 12 to 15 minutes, until the filling is set. Remove from the oven and cool on a wire rack.

MAKES 10 TARTLETS

Lattice Tart with Fresh Berry Filling

A *golden brown lattice shows off any tart filling nicely and it's much easier than it looks. The final brushing with egg and granulated sugar, performed with a delicate hand, will give your pastry a glow.*

1 RECIPE PASTRY FOR DOUBLE-CRUST PIE (PAGE 155)

1 CUP SUGAR, PLUS ADDITIONAL FOR DUSTING

⅓ CUP ALL-PURPOSE FLOUR

4 CUPS FRESH BERRIES (RASPBERRIES, BLUEBERRIES, BLACKBERRIES, OR BOYSENBERRIES)

2 TABLESPOONS (¼ STICK) UNSALTED BUTTER

1 EGG, LIGHTLY BEATEN

CONFECTIONERS' SUGAR, FOR DUSTING

Prepare the pastry according to the directions on page 155. Divide the dough in half and form each half into a ball. On a lightly floured surface, use your palm to slightly flatten one ball of the dough. Using a floured rolling pin, roll the dough out from the center to the edge into a 12-inch circle.

To transfer the pastry to a tart pan, wrap it around the rolling pin. Unroll the pastry into a 9-inch tart pan with a removable bottom. Roll the remaining dough into a 12-inch circle and set aside.

Preheat the oven to 425°F.

In a large mixing bowl, stir together the granulated sugar and flour. Gently stir in the berries and toss well. Spoon into the pastry-lined tart pan and dot with the butter.

To form the lattice top, cut the remaining pastry circle into ten strips. Lay half of the pastry strips in one direction across the filling; lay the other half of the strips in the other direction. Press the ends of the strips into the crust rim. Fold the bottom pastry over the strips and seal.

Brush the lattice top with the beaten egg and sprinkle with the granulated sugar. Place the tart on a baking sheet and bake for 40 to 45 minutes, or until the crust is golden brown. Remove from the oven and cool completely on a wire rack.

To serve, dust with sifted confectioners' sugar.

SERVES 8

Linzer Torte with Fresh Raspberries

It was a customer who came up with the idea of using fresh raspberries on our Linzer Torte. We make ours with an authentic Linzer dough and raspberry jam, reminiscent of the traditional Austrian treat. But by crowning the torte with fresh berries, the fruit flavor is heightened, giving this classic a new twist.

⅔ CUP LIGHTLY ROASTED HAZELNUTS (SEE NOTE)

1¼ CUPS ALL-PURPOSE FLOUR

½ TEASPOON GROUND CINNAMON

¼ TEASPOON SALT

¼ TEASPOON BAKING POWDER

6 TABLESPOONS (¾ STICK) UNSALTED BUTTER, SOFTENED

⅓ CUP FIRMLY PACKED LIGHT BROWN SUGAR

1 EGG

½ TEASPOON VANILLA EXTRACT

1 CUP RASPBERRY PRESERVES

8 OUNCES FRESH RASPBERRIES

CONFECTIONERS' SUGAR, FOR DUSTING

In the bowl of a food processor, blend together the hazelnuts with ¼ cup of the flour for 30 seconds, or until the hazelnuts are finely ground. Add the remaining flour, cinnamon, salt, and baking powder and process for 10 to 15 seconds, until thoroughly blended.

In a mixing bowl on medium speed, beat the butter for 30 seconds, or until creamy. Add the light brown sugar and continue beating for 2 to 3 minutes. Scrape down the sides of the bowl with a rubber spatula. Beat in the egg and the vanilla.

On low speed, beat in the flour mixture, one-third at a time, scraping down the sides of the bowl after each addition.

With floured hands, press three-fourths of the dough onto the bottom and up the sides of a 9-inch tart pan with removable bottom. Trim the edge even with the rim of the pan. Wrap the tart shell and remaining dough in plastic wrap and refrigerate for 30 minutes, or until the dough is firm enough to roll.

Preheat the oven to 375°F.

Spoon the raspberry preserves into the chilled tart shell. Bake the tart for 30 to 35 minutes, or until the filling is hot and bubbly and the crust is nicely browned. Cool the tart on a wire rack for at least 1 hour.

On a well-floured surface, using a floured rolling pin, roll out the remaining dough to ⅛-inch thickness. Using a 1-inch star cookie cutter, cut out the cookies. Using a spatula, transfer the cookies to an ungreased baking sheet, leaving about 1 inch between them.

Bake the cookies for 8 to 10 minutes, or until the edges are just starting to turn brown. Cool on the baking sheet on a wire rack for 1 minute. Using a metal spatula, transfer the cookies to a wire rack to cool completely.

Arrange the raspberries, pointed end up, over the cooled raspberry filling. Garnish with Linzer star cookies.

To serve, dust with sifted confectioners' sugar.

SERVES 8

NOTE: To roast hazelnuts, position a rack in the center of the oven and preheat to 350°F. Spread the hazelnuts in a single layer on a baking sheet and roast for 8 to 12 minutes, shaking the pan 2 or 3 times until the nuts are golden beneath their skins. Wrap the nuts in a clean towel and cool completely. Transfer the nuts to a large strainer and rub them back and forth to remove the loose skins.

Old-Fashioned Pear Crisp with Ginger

$\mathbf{F}$*or this recipe I like to use moist pears like Anjou, which are particularly fragrant, or Bosc, which have a firm texture. The secret to this recipe is Poire William, a delicious pear brandy that adds a sparkle and really complements the ginger. Serve the crisp warm with a dollop of whipped cream or a big scoop of your favorite ice cream.*

Fruit Filling

6 LARGE RIPE PEARS (3 POUNDS) PEELED, CORED, AND THINLY SLICED (ABOUT 10 CUPS)

¼ CUP PURE MAPLE SYRUP

1 TABLESPOON FRESH LEMON JUICE

1 TABLESPOON POIRE WILLIAM PEAR BRANDY

1 TEASPOON GROUND ALLSPICE

Gingersnap Topping

½ CUP FIRMLY PACKED LIGHT BROWN SUGAR

½ CUP ALL-PURPOSE FLOUR

¼ TEASPOON GROUND CINNAMON

6 TABLESPOONS (¾ STICK) UNSALTED BUTTER, CUT INTO SMALL PIECES AND CHILLED

½ CUP COARSELY CRUSHED GINGERSNAP COOKIES

½ CUP FINELY CHOPPED PECANS

2 TABLESPOONS FINELY CHOPPED CANDIED GINGER

Preheat the oven to 425°F.

In a large bowl combine the pears, maple syrup, lemon juice, brandy, and allspice. Spoon the mixture into a shallow 2-quart 11 × 7-inch baking pan.

In another large bowl, combine the brown sugar, flour, and cinnamon. Using a pastry blender or two knives, cut in the butter until the mixture resembles coarse meal. Stir in the crushed gingersnaps, pecans, and candied ginger, and sprinkle the mixture evenly over the fruit.

Bake for 10 minutes. Reduce the oven temperature to 350°F. and bake for an additional 30 minutes, or until the top is golden brown and the fruit is bubbly and tender. Serve warm.

SERVES 8

Mini Cream Puffs

If I had a nickel for every time somebody came into the bakery, looked at these mini cream puffs, and said, "I can remember when cream puffs were a nickel," well, I'd have a lot of nickels. We developed these mini cream puffs, drizzled with chocolate, for our catering menu, but they're great for an everyday dessert or a snack. If you like, you can substitute chocolate mousse or your favorite ice cream for the custard.

Cream Puff Pastry

6 TABLESPOONS (¾ STICK) UNSALTED BUTTER, CUT INTO PIECES

¼ TEASPOON SALT

1 CUP ALL-PURPOSE FLOUR

1 CUP EGGS, LIGHTLY BEATEN (ABOUT 5 LARGE EGGS)

1 RECIPE CUSTARD FILLING (PAGE XX)

8 OUNCES GOOD-QUALITY SEMISWEET CHOCOLATE, MELTED AND COOLED

CONFECTIONERS' SUGAR, FOR DUSTING

Preheat the oven to 400° F. Grease a baking sheet.

In a medium saucepan over medium heat, combine 1 cup water, the butter, and salt and bring to a boil. Add the flour all at once and mix well. Cook, stirring constantly, until the mixture forms a ball that does not separate, about 2 minutes. Remove from the heat and cool for 10 minutes. Add the egg in increments of five, beating well with a wooden spoon after each addition so that the pastry absorbs each addition of egg. The pastry should just hold its shape when lifted with a spoon.

Spoon the batter into a pastry bag fitted with a large plain round tip (1-inch opening). Pipe the batter into round mounds 1 inch high onto the prepared baking sheet, leaving about 1½ inches between each piece.

Bake for 20 to 25 minutes, until the puffs are a nice golden brown and crisp to touch. Rapidly remove from the oven, turn off the heat, and make a small slash in each puff to let out some steam. Then return to the oven for 5 minutes. Remove and cool completely on a wire rack.

Using a serrated knife, slice the top off each puff. Fill a pastry bag without a tip with the custard filling and pipe about 2 tablespoons into the bottom half of each puff. Cover with the top of the puff and drizzle with melted chocolate. Dust with confectioners' sugar and serve.

MAKES ABOUT 24 MINI CREAM PUFFS

Lemon Meringue Pie

¶ *learned the hard way that a meringue needs well-beaten egg whites or it will fall as soon as it comes out of the oven. When I was fifteen years old, I whipped up enough meringue for twenty-four pies. I thought the whites were stiff enough, but I guess they weren't, because every last one fell down flat—and there was nothing I could do except start over. If you're making meringue, whip the egg whites until they are very stiff. This recipe comes with an extra bit of insurance: the sponge cake layer, which gives the pie a lovely flavor and texture and soaks up the excess liquid if the meringue starts to weep.*

1 RECIPE PASTRY FOR SINGLE-CRUST PIE (PAGE 156)

Lemon Filling

1⅓ CUPS SUGAR

½ CUP CORNSTARCH

¼ TEASPOON SALT

4 EGG YOLKS

2 TABLESPOONS (¼ STICK) UNSALTED BUTTER

1 TABLESPOON GRATED LEMON ZEST

½ CUP FRESH LEMON JUICE

1 RECIPE SPONGE CAKE (PAGE 152)

Meringue

4 EGG WHITES

¼ TEASPOON CREAM OF TARTAR

½ CUP SUGAR

Prepare and roll out the pastry according to the directions on page 156. Trim and flute the edges as desired. Preheat the oven to 450° F. Prick the bottom and sides of the pastry in the pie plate with a fork.

Line the pastry with a double thickness of foil and bake for 8 minutes. Remove the foil and continue baking for 5 to 6 minutes, or until golden brown. Cool completely on a wire rack.

In a medium saucepan, combine the sugar, cornstarch, and salt. Gradually blend in 1¾ cups water and cook over medium heat, stirring constantly, until the mixture thickens and bubbles, about 4 minutes. Remove from the heat.

In a small bowl, whisk the egg yolks slightly. Beat in a small amount of the sugar mixture, then gradually beat the egg yolk mixture into the sugar mixture. Cook over low heat, stirring constantly, for 2 minutes (do not boil). Remove from the heat and stir in the butter, lemon zest, and lemon juice. Transfer the mixture to a bowl and cover the surface with plastic wrap. Refrigerate until chilled, about 2 hours.

Pour the chilled lemon filling into the prepared shell. Cut the sponge cake in half horizontally, forming two equal layers. Top the lemon filling with one sponge cake layer. Freeze the remaining layer for another use (see Note).

Preheat the oven to 400° F.

In a small mixing bowl, beat the egg whites with the cream of tartar until foamy. Add the sugar, one tablespoon at a time, and continue beating until the egg whites form stiff peaks. Using a pastry bag fitted with a large star tip, pipe the meringue in mounds over the sponge cake in the pie shell. To prevent the meringue from shrinking, pipe around the edge of the pie, making sure the meringue touches the crust.

Bake for 5 to 10 minutes, or until the meringue is golden brown. Cool completely on a wire rack, then refrigerate 4 hours before serving.

SERVES 8

NOTE: Extra sponge cake can be cut into small pieces and layered with pudding or mousse, fresh fruit, or ice cream. Or make into cake crumbs and use as a topping.

Pecan Pie

Here's a traditional Southern favorite—Southern Brooklyn, that is. Chock-full of pecans, it has a deliciously gooey, sweet filling created by layering sugar, honey, and corn syrup. Serve it warm or cold with ice cream or hot fudge. If you're feeling daring (or if you don't happen to have pecans), you can substitute walnuts for the pecans.

1 RECIPE PASTRY FOR SINGLE-CRUST PIE (PAGE 156)

3 EGGS

1 CUP SUGAR

½ CUP HONEY

½ CUP LIGHT CORN SYRUP

1 TEASPOON VANILLA EXTRACT

1½ CUPS PECAN HALVES

Prepare and roll out the pastry according to the directions on page 156. Line a 9-inch pie plate with the pastry. Trim and flute the edges as desired and set aside.

Preheat the oven to 350°F.

In a medium bowl, beat the eggs slightly. Add the sugar, honey, corn syrup, and vanilla and mix until well combined. Stir in the pecans. Pour the filling into the piecrust.

Bake for 50 to 55 minutes, or until the filling is golden and puffy and a knife inserted halfway between the center and the edge comes out clean. Cool completely on a wire rack.

SERVES 8

Breads

Chocolate Babka
with Streusel Topping

*T*his is my partner Joel's favorite cake. We call him the Babka Monster—Great Neck's answer to Sesame Street's Cookie Monster. He often sets one aside in the morning to take home at the end of the day, but sometimes, when a customer comes in looking for chocolate babka after we've sold the last one in the case, he'll hand over his. Anything for our customers! Savor this babka as a dessert or as an indulgent breakfast pastry, or eat it as a treat with your coffee break. Whatever the time of day, you'll enjoy the crumbly streusel topping and chocolate swirl inside. It's as delicious toasted and buttered as it is fresh.

Babka Dough

1½ CUPS WARM (105° TO 110°F.) WATER

3 ¼-OUNCE PACKAGES ACTIVE DRY YEAST (2 TABLESPOONS)

¾ CUP SUGAR

2 EGGS

2 EGG YOLKS

1 TABLESPOON GRATED ORANGE ZEST

1 TABLESPOON VANILLA EXTRACT

1 TEASPOON SALT

⅓ CUP NON-FAT DRY MILK POWDER

1 CUP (2 STICKS) UNSALTED BUTTER,
    SOFTENED AND CUT INTO SMALL PIECES

6½ CUPS BREAD FLOUR

Chocolate Filling

½ CUP SUGAR

1 TABLESPOON GROUND CINNAMON

8 OUNCES GOOD-QUALITY SEMISWEET CHOCOLATE,
    MELTED AND COOLED

Streusel Topping

½ CUP (1 STICK) UNSALTED BUTTER, DIVIDED

¾ CUP ALL-PURPOSE FLOUR

½ CUP FIRMLY PACKED LIGHT BROWN SUGAR

In a large mixing bowl, whisk together the warm water, yeast, and 1 teaspoon of the granulated sugar. Let the mixture stand for 5 minutes, until bubbly.

Stir in the eggs, egg yolks, orange zest, vanilla, remaining granulated sugar, salt, and dry milk powder and mix well. Stir in the softened butter and 3 cups of the flour, then add the remaining 3½ cups of flour. Turn the dough out onto a work surface and knead for 8 to 10 minutes, until the flour is incorporated and the dough is smooth and elastic. Shape into a ball. Place in a greased bowl, turning the dough to grease the surface. Cover the dough with a dish towel and let rise in a warm place until doubled in size, 1 to 1½ hours.

Punch the dough down and turn out onto a lightly floured surface. Divide the dough in half, cover with a dish towel, and let rest for 10 minutes.

In a small bowl, combine the granulated sugar and cinnamon for the chocolate filling and set aside.

continued on next page

Preheat the oven to 350° F. Generously grease two 9-inch spring-form or layer cake pans. Roll half of the dough into a 16-inch square. Spread with half of the melted chocolate and sprinkle with half of the sugar-cinnamon mixture. Roll up jelly roll style and place the dough, seam-side down, into the prepared pan, bringing the ends together and pinching the ends to seal. Repeat with the remaining dough and filling ingredients.

Place the pans in a plastic bag and let the dough rise until it is nearly doubled in size, about 1 hour.

To prepare the streusel topping, melt 2 tablespoons of the butter and set aside. In a medium bowl, combine the flour and brown sugar. With a fork or pastry blender, cut in the remaining 6 tablespoons of butter until the mixture is crumbly.

Using a pastry brush, brush the top of the babkas with the melted butter. Sprinkle each babka with half of the streusel topping. Bake for 35 to 45 minutes, or until the top of the babka is medium brown. Cool in the pan for 15 minutes, then transfer to wire racks and cool completely.

MAKES 2 BABKAS TO SERVE 24

Scones

*O*n Election Day one year, we thought it would be fun to host breakfast for Great Neck's Democrats and Republicans. We divided the restaurant in half and sat each party on one side. I hosted the Democrats and my partner Joel hosted the Republicans, and we got them to agree on at least one thing: These scones are delicious! Better still, they are easy and quick to make. A word of caution: Avoid overworking the dough or the scones will come out too smooth.

4 CUPS ALL-PURPOSE FLOUR

1 CUP PLUS 3 TABLESPOONS SUGAR

2 TEASPOONS BAKING POWDER

1 TEASPOON SALT

1¼ CUPS (2½ STICKS) UNSALTED BUTTER, CUT INTO SMALL PIECES

1 CUP DRIED CURRANTS

1 EGG

¾ CUP HEAVY CREAM

Preheat the oven to 400° F. Grease a large baking sheet.

In a mixing bowl combine the flour, sugar, baking powder, and salt. Using a pastry blender, cut in the butter and blend until the mixture resembles coarse crumbs. Stir in the currants. Add the egg and heavy cream and stir to combine. Knead the dough in the mixing bowl until smooth, about 3 minutes. Do not overwork.

Turn the dough out on a lightly floured surface and roll into a rectangle approximately 1 inch thick. Using a 3-inch round biscuit cutter, cut out the scones and place on the prepared baking sheet.

Bake for 14 to 18 minutes, or until golden brown. Remove the scones from the baking sheet and serve warm.

MAKES 12 TO 15 SCONES

Mandelbrot

At Bruce's Bakery, we like to slice our mandelbrot and offer samples to our patrons, who like it so much they sometimes ask for seconds. "Mandelbrot" is a German-Jewish word that means "almond bread." But this crunchy treat is more like Italian biscotti to me. Our version is flavored with almond paste, enriched with farmer cheese, and loaded with chocolate chips and for good measure, a ribbon of melted chocolate that runs straight through the middle.

4 OUNCES ALMOND PASTE

1 CUP SUGAR

²/₃ CUP VEGETABLE SHORTENING

3 OUNCES FARMER CHEESE

2 EGGS

2 EGG YOLKS

2 TEASPOONS VANILLA EXTRACT

2 TEASPOONS ALMOND EXTRACT

3½ CUPS ALL-PURPOSE FLOUR

1 TEASPOON BAKING POWDER

½ TEASPOON BAKING SODA

½ TEASPOON SALT

¼ CUP MILK

2 CUPS SEMISWEET CHOCOLATE CHIPS

3 OUNCES SEMISWEET CHOCOLATE, MELTED AND COOLED

Topping

2 TABLESPOONS FINELY CHOPPED WALNUTS

1½ TABLESPOONS SUGAR

¼ TEASPOON GROUND CINNAMON

1 EGG, LIGHTLY BEATEN

Preheat the oven to 350° F. Line a baking sheet with parchment paper.

Using a grater or food processor, grate or shred the almond paste into a large mixing bowl. Add the sugar and mix well on low speed. Add the shortening and farmer cheese and continue beating until smooth. Add the eggs and egg yolks, one at a time, mixing well after each addition, then add the vanilla and almond extracts and beat until blended.

In a separate bowl, combine the flour, baking powder, baking soda, and salt. Gradually add the flour mixture to the batter, alternating with the milk, until well combined. Stir in the chocolate chips. Place the dough on a lightly floured cutting board and drizzle with the melted chocolate. Using floured hands (the dough will be sticky), knead the dough, incorporating the drizzled chocolate and creating a marbleized effect. In a small bowl, combine the chopped nuts, sugar, and cinnamon.

Divide the dough into three equal pieces. Form each piece into an oval football shape about 6 inches long. Place on the prepared baking sheet and brush with the beaten egg. Sprinkle with the topping mixture.

Bake 45 to 55 minutes, until the dough is richly golden and seems dry to the touch. Remove from the oven and cool completely on a wire rack. Using a serrated knife, cut each log into ¾-inch slices.

MAKES 3 MANDELBROT TO SERVE 30

Irish Soda Bread

The aroma of Irish Soda Bread emanating from the oven triggers such great memories for me. Working with my father at his bakery, we made it only once a year, for St. Patrick's Day. There's something about the combination of caraway and sweet currants that I associate with spring training and the opening day of baseball. To me it says, "Let's play ball."

1 CUP WHOLE-WHEAT FLOUR

1 CUP ALL-PURPOSE FLOUR

1½ TEASPOONS BAKING POWDER

½ TEASPOON BAKING SODA

½ TEASPOON SALT

2 TABLESPOONS FIRMLY PACKED LIGHT BROWN SUGAR

¼ CUP VEGETABLE SHORTENING, CHILLED

2 EGGS

⅔ CUP BUTTERMILK

¾ CUP CURRANTS

1 TABLESPOON CARAWAY SEEDS

Preheat the oven to 375° F. Lightly grease an 8-inch round baking pan and set aside.

In a medium-size mixing bowl, stir together the whole-wheat flour, all-purpose flour, baking powder, baking soda, salt, and brown sugar. Using a pastry blender or two knives, cut in the shortening until the mixture resembles coarse meal. Make a well in the center of the mixture and set aside.

In a small bowl, combine 1 egg, the buttermilk, currants, and caraway seeds. Add the egg mixture all at once to the dry mixture and stir just until moistened.

On a lightly floured surface using floured hands, quickly knead the dough by folding and gently pressing the dough for 10 to 12 strokes, or until the dough is nearly smooth. Shape into a round loaf and place into the prepared pan.

Lightly beat the remaining egg and brush it on the loaf. Bake the loaf for 35 to 40 minutes, or until golden brown. Serve warm.

SERVES 8

Frostings, Fillings, and Puddings

Blackout Cream

This is our own special recipe for blackout cream, a sweet, creamy, comfort-food pudding with the grown-up taste of dark chocolate. It's an essential ingredient in our Blackout Cake (page 54), but you can also use it for any layer cake—or grab a spoon and eat it alone or with whipped cream.

½ CUP SUGAR

2 TABLESPOONS LIGHT CORN SYRUP

10 OUNCES GOOD-QUALITY SEMISWEET CHOCOLATE,
   COARSELY CHOPPED

¼ CUP CORNSTARCH

¼ CUP HEAVY CREAM

4 TABLESPOONS (½ STICK) UNSALTED BUTTER,
   CUT INTO PIECES

In a medium saucepan over low heat, combine 1½ cups of water, the sugar, and corn syrup. Stir in the chocolate and cook, stirring constantly, until the chocolate is melted, about 2 to 3 minutes.

In a small bowl, combine ½ cup of water and the cornstarch and whisk until the cornstarch is dissolved. Add the dissolved cornstarch paste and the heavy cream to the chocolate mixture and bring to a boil, stirring constantly. Boil for 1 minute. Remove from the heat and whisk in the butter.

Transfer the mixture to a bowl. Cover the surface with plastic wrap and chill for 1 hour before serving.

MAKES 2½ CUPS

(ENOUGH TO FILL AND FROST A 2-LAYER CAKE)

Chocolate Mousse

In the past twenty years, chocolate mousse has become a standard bakery item, but when it first became popular in the 1970s, it was considered exotic. Some bakers tried to pass off chocolate whipped cream as mousse, but it isn't the same: Real chocolate mousse is richer and denser. This combination of whipped heavy cream and pure chocolate is so rich that a little goes a long way. Terrific alone, it can be used as a cake filling or topping as well. It's the food of the gods—the chocolate gods, at any rate.

8 OUNCES GOOD-QUALITY SEMISWEET CHOCOLATE, COARSELY CHOPPED

2 TABLESPOONS (¼ STICK) UNSALTED BUTTER

1 CUP HEAVY CREAM

1 TABLESPOON SUGAR

1 TEASPOON VANILLA EXTRACT

In a medium saucepan over low heat, combine the chocolate, butter, and ⅔ cup of the heavy cream, stirring until the chocolate is melted and the mixture is smooth, about 3 to 4 minutes. Scrape the mixture into a bowl and let cool to room temperature.

In a mixing bowl, beat the remaining ⅓ cup of heavy cream, the sugar, and vanilla until stiff peaks form. Gently fold a small amount of the whipped cream into the cooled chocolate mixture. Using a rubber spatula, fold in the remaining whipped cream. Spoon the mousse into six individual goblets or dessert dishes or one large bowl. Refrigerate for at least 1 hour before serving.

MAKES ABOUT 2 CUPS

Chocolate Bread Pudding

Bread pudding is a comfort dessert that can be transported into luxury—just with the addition of chocolate. Cubes of bread, baked in a chocolate custard, rise to the top, creating a crusty, irresistible treat.

1 FRENCH BAGUETTE (ABOUT 10 OUNCES)

8 OUNCES GOOD-QUALITY BITTERSWEET CHOCOLATE, FINELY CHOPPED

1 CUP HEAVY CREAM

1 TEASPOON VANILLA EXTRACT

3 EGGS

½ CUP SOUR CREAM

½ CUP SUGAR

¼ TEASPOON GROUND CINNAMON

WHIPPED CREAM

Preheat the oven to 325° F. Lightly grease the bottom and sides of six 6-ounce ramekins or soufflé dishes and set aside.

Using a serrated knife, remove the crusts from the baguette. Cut the bread into ½-inch cubes and spread in a single layer on a baking sheet. Toast for 5 to 10 minutes, or until lightly browned and crisp. Cool the bread on the baking sheet on a wire rack.

Place the chocolate in a medium bowl. In a small saucepan over medium heat, bring ½ cup of the cream to a gentle boil. Pour the hot cream over the chocolate. Let stand for 30 seconds to melt the chocolate. Gently whisk until smooth. Stir in the vanilla.

In a large bowl, whisk together the remaining ½ cup heavy cream, eggs, sour cream, sugar, cinnamon, and chocolate mixture. Add the toasted bread cubes and set aside for 2 hours, or until the bread soaks up the chocolate custard.

Place the ramekins in a 13 × 9 × 2-inch baking pan and place in the preheated oven. Pour boiling water into the baking pan until it comes halfway up the sides of the ramekins. Bake the puddings for 25 to 30 minutes or until a toothpick inserted in the center comes out clean. Using a pancake spatula, carefully remove the puddings from the pan of water.

Garnish each pudding with a dollop of whipped cream and serve immediately.

SERVES 6

Buttercream

The secret to a good buttercream is the blending—and in the bakery, that's quite a proposition, because we make it in 120-quart vats. When I was a kid, the process was mechanized, but every so often, you'd have to stop the machine and scrape down the mixture that had become stuck to the sides of the vat. I was just fourteen when I started doing this chore, and I had to stand on a milk crate in order to be able to reach into the vat—I was lucky I didn't fall in headfirst! A few years later I could reach it standing on the floor like all the other bakers. True to its name, this pastry-shop favorite is buttery, luscious, and absolutely perfect for frosting and decorating all kinds of cakes. If you have more than you can use, remember that it freezes well (up to 3 months) and can be thawed overnight in the refrigerator or over several hours at room temperature.

6 EGG YOLKS

1 CUP PLUS 2 TABLESPOONS SUGAR

2 CUPS (4 STICKS) UNSALTED BUTTER, SOFTENED

2 TABLESPOONS VANILLA EXTRACT

In a large mixing bowl, beat the egg yolks on medium-high speed until light in color and tripled in volume, about 7 minutes. While the eggs are mixing, prepare the sugar syrup.

In a small saucepan, combine the sugar and ½ cup water. Cook over medium heat, stirring constantly, until the sugar dissolves, about 2 minutes. Increase the heat to medium-high and bring the mixture to a boil. Continue to boil, unstirred, for about 12 minutes, until the mixture reaches the soft-ball stage (238°F. on a candy thermometer). Remove the pan from the heat and pour a small amount of the syrup over the egg yolks. Beat with an electric mixer on high speed for 5 seconds. Turn off the mixer, add more syrup, and beat again. Continue this process, gradually adding the remaining syrup and continuing to beat, for 5 minutes, until the mixture is cool.

Once the mixture has cooled, lower the speed and gradually add the butter 2 tablespoons at a time. Add the vanilla and combine well.

Transfer the buttercream to a clean bowl and cover with plastic wrap. If you are planning to use it on the same day, set it aside at room temperature for up to 6 hours. The buttercream may be made a few days in advance and stored in the refrigerator. Before using, let it come to room temperature so it will be soft enough to spread.

MAKES ABOUT 4 CUPS

Chocolate Buttercream

Buttercream is the workhorse of the bakery. We use it to ice cakes and create all kinds of decorations, and we flavor it in many ways, chocolate being one of the most popular. This recipe calls for melted bittersweet chocolate and Cognac, but you can use semisweet or milk chocolate or a combination. Or add a few drops of chocolate liqueur. The buttercream absorbs the chocolate beautifully. And it's absolutely delicious.

6 EGG YOLKS

1 CUP PLUS 2 TABLESPOONS SUGAR

2 CUPS (4 STICKS) UNSALTED BUTTER, SOFTENED

10 OUNCES GOOD-QUALITY BITTERSWEET CHOCOLATE, MELTED AND COOLED

2 TABLESPOONS COGNAC OR CHOCOLATE-FLAVORED LIQUEUR (OPTIONAL)

In a large mixing bowl, beat the egg yolks on medium-high speed until light in color and tripled in volume, about 7 minutes.

In a small saucepan, combine the sugar and ½ cup water. Cook over medium heat, stirring constantly, until the sugar dissolves. Increase the heat to medium-high and bring the mixture to a boil. Continue to boil, unstirred, for about 12 minutes, until the mixture reaches the soft-ball stage (238° F. on a candy thermometer). Remove the pan from the heat and pour a small amount of the syrup over the egg yolks. Beat with an electric mixer on high speed for 5 seconds. Turn the mixer off, add more syrup, and beat again. Continue this process, gradually adding the remaining syrup and continuing to beat, for 5 minutes, until the mixture is cool.

Once the mixture is cooled, lower the speed and gradually add the butter, 2 tablespoons at a time. Add the melted chocolate and Cognac and beat until combined.

Transfer the buttercream to a clean bowl and cover with plastic wrap. If you are planning to use the buttercream on the same day, set it aside at room temperature for up to 6 hours. The buttercream may be made a few days in advance and stored in the refrigerator. Before using, let it come to room temperature so it will be soft enough to spread.

MAKES ABOUT 4 CUPS

Coffee Buttercream

The coffee that goes into this recipe can be reinforced by a tablespoon or two of coffee liqueur. You'll be surprised at the real coffee flavor that results. That's the great thing about buttercream: You can flavor it any way you want. At Bruce's we do a Fantasy Island Cake, which is decorated with a bouquet of all kinds of brightly colored buttercream flowers. You can use coffee, chocolate, or any fruit-flavored liqueur.

2 TEASPOONS ESPRESSO OR INSTANT COFFEE GRANULES

1 TABLESPOON WARM WATER

6 EGG YOLKS

1 CUP PLUS 2 TABLESPOONS SUGAR

2 CUPS (4 STICKS) UNSALTED BUTTER, SOFTENED

1 TABLESPOON COFFEE-FLAVORED LIQUEUR, SUCH AS TIA MARIA

In a small bowl, dissolve the espresso in the warm water and set aside.

In a large mixing bowl, beat the egg yolks on medium-high speed until light in color and tripled in volume, about 7 minutes. While the eggs are mixing, prepare the syrup.

In a small saucepan, combine the sugar and ½ cup water. Cook over medium heat, stirring constantly, until the sugar dissolves, about 2 minutes. Increase the heat to medium-high and bring the mixture to a boil. Continue to boil, unstirred, for about 12 minutes, until the mixture reaches the soft-ball stage (238° F. on a candy thermometer). Remove the pan from the heat and pour a small amount of the syrup over the egg yolks. Beat with an electric mixer on high speed for 5 seconds. Turn the mixer off, add more syrup, and beat again. Continue this process, gradually adding the remaining syrup and continuing to beat, for 5 minutes, until the mixture is cool.

Once the mixture has cooled, lower the speed and gradually add the butter 2 tablespoons at a time. Add the dissolved espresso and coffee liqueur and combine well.

Transfer the buttercream to a clean bowl and cover with plastic wrap. If you are planning to use it on the same day, set it aside at room temperature for up to 6 hours. The buttercream may be made a few days in advance and stored in the refrigerator. Before using, let it come to room temperature so it will be soft enough to spread.

MAKES 4 CUPS

Cream Cheese Frosting

A good cream cheese frosting is creamy, rich, and smooth, and in my opinion, a touch of orange really enhances the flavor. It's a perfect complement for carrot cake, spice cake, date nut bread, tea cake or bread, or even pound cake. Be careful not to overbeat, or the frosting will come out grainy and thin.

1 8-OUNCE PACKAGE CREAM CHEESE, SOFTENED

½ CUP (1 STICK) UNSALTED BUTTER, SOFTENED

2 TEASPOONS VANILLA EXTRACT

1 TEASPOON GRATED ORANGE ZEST

3 CUPS CONFECTIONERS' SUGAR

In a large mixing bowl on low speed, beat the cream cheese, butter, vanilla, and orange zest until light and fluffy, about 2 minutes. Gradually add the confectioners' sugar and beat well.

MAKES 2½ CUPS

(ENOUGH TO FILL AND FROST A 2-LAYER CAKE)

Fudge Icing

*K*ids *love this fudge icing and ask for it on their birthday cakes year after year. You can use it on any kind of cake as a frosting or filling. Or use it to ice cookies or make sandwich cookies. You can store this in the refrigerator for a week to ten days or freeze it for three to four weeks. If you keep it chilled, it travels exceptionally well.*

2/3 CUP UNSWEETENED COCOA POWDER

2/3 CUP UNSALTED BUTTER, SOFTENED

1 1-POUND PACKAGE CONFECTIONERS' SUGAR (ABOUT 3¾ CUPS)

1 TABLESPOON VANILLA EXTRACT

2 TO 4 TABLESPOONS HOT WATER

In a large mixing bowl, combine the cocoa and butter. Beating on low speed, gradually add the confectioners' sugar. Beat in the vanilla and hot water until the frosting is smooth and reaches spreadable consistency, about 2 minutes.

MAKES ABOUT 2 1/2 CUPS

(ENOUGH TO FILL AND FROST A 2-LAYER CAKE)

Custard Filling

*M*y daughter Ryann adores custard; sometimes she'll ask me to bring home a custard treat. She has a lot to choose from because we use this filling for eclairs, doughnuts, danish, pies, tarts, tartlets, and layer cakes. For the pies, tarts, and cakes, you can top the custard with sliced fresh strawberries, bananas, or other fruit, or mix the fruit into the custard. For a little extra zip, you can blend in a tablespoon of fruit liqueur.

6 EGG YOLKS

½ CUP SUGAR

½ TEASPOON SALT

½ CUP ALL-PURPOSE FLOUR

2 CUPS MILK OR HALF-AND-HALF, HEATED

1 TABLESPOON VANILLA EXTRACT

1 TABLESPOON FRUIT LIQUEUR (OPTIONAL)

2 TABLESPOONS (¼ STICK) UNSALTED BUTTER

½ CUP HEAVY CREAM

In a medium saucepan over low heat, whisk the egg yolks, gradually beating in the sugar and salt. Continue whisking for 2 to 3 minutes, until the mixture is thick and lemon colored. Sift in the flour, then gradually add the heated milk, stirring to combine.

Set the pan over medium heat, continuing to whisk slowly. As the mixture comes to a boil, stir constantly, using a wooden spoon. Cook for 2 minutes.

Remove from the heat and blend in the vanilla, fruit liqueur, if using, and butter. Pass the filling through a fine mesh sieve set over a large bowl; cool. Cover the surface with plastic wrap and refrigerate for several hours until ready to serve.

Before serving, beat the heavy cream in a small mixing bowl for about 2 minutes, until stiff peaks form. Gently fold the cream into the custard filling.

MAKES 2 1/2 CUPS

Chocolate Ganache

*M*aking chocolate ganache was one of my jobs when I worked in my dad's bakery while I was going to college. It's a simple process that yields an incredibly elegant result: Blend the best chocolate you can find with a heated mixture of sugar and heavy cream and you get a frosting that's sinfully delicious. Use it on cakes, brownies, or cookies. Leftover ganache keeps beautifully in the refrigerator for a week or in the freezer for several months.

16 OUNCES GOOD-QUALITY SEMISWEET CHOCOLATE, FINELY CHOPPED

1 CUP HEAVY CREAM

3/4 CUP SUGAR

Place the chopped chocolate in a large mixing bowl. In a small saucepan over medium heat, bring the heavy cream and sugar to a boil, stirring until the sugar is dissolved. Pour the heated cream mixture over the chocolate and let it sit for 1 minute. With a wooden spoon, stir until the chocolate is melted and the mixture is smooth. Let set until slightly thickened, about 15 minutes.

MAKES ABOUT 2 1/2 CUPS

Master
Recipes

White Layer Cake

If there's one thing I can't stand it's a white layer cake that has the feel of dried-out foam rubber. Plain white cake deserves our respect—the best ingredients and the utmost care. This white cake is one of the most tender, moistest white cakes you'll ever eat. It goes equally well with Buttercream (pages 136 and 138) or Fudge Icing (page 143).

1 CUP SIFTED CAKE FLOUR

1 TEASPOON BAKING POWDER

¼ TEASPOON SALT

6 EGGS, SEPARATED, YOLKS AND WHITES RESERVED

¾ CUP PLUS 2 TABLESPOONS SUGAR

1 TEASPOON VANILLA EXTRACT

6 TABLESPOONS (¾ STICK) UNSALTED BUTTER, MELTED

½ TEASPOON CREAM OF TARTAR

Preheat the oven to 350° F. Grease and flour a 9-inch springform pan. Line the bottom of the pan with parchment paper or wax paper. Grease the paper and set aside.

In a medium-size bowl, sift together the cake flour, baking powder, and salt.

In another mixing bowl, beat the egg yolks on high speed until thick and lemon colored, about 5 minutes. Reduce the speed to low and gradually beat in ¾ cup of the sugar. Continue beating until the mixture thickens slightly and doubles in volume, about 5 minutes. Beat in the vanilla.

Sift ⅓ cup of the flour mixture over the egg yolk mixture and gently fold it in until combined. Repeat with ⅓-cup measures of the remaining flour mixture. Blend in the melted butter.

In a mixing bowl, beat the egg whites and cream of tartar on medium speed until soft peaks form. Gradually add the remaining 2 tablespoons of sugar, beating on high speed until stiff peaks form. Gently fold the egg whites into the batter.

Spoon the batter into the prepared pan. Bake for 25 to 30 minutes, or until the center springs back when lightly touched. Cool on a wire rack for 10 minutes. Remove from the pan and cool completely.

SERVES 12

Chocolate Layer Cake

*M*y son Jared loves my intensely chocolate layer cake. As soon as I bring him a piece, he dips his finger into the fudge icing and takes a taste. Then he tastes the chocolate cake and delivers his verdict. Sometimes I frost it with a traditional chocolate fudge frosting and sometimes I surprise him with a contrasting flavor. Either way, you can't go wrong.

6 EGGS, SEPARATED, YOLKS AND WHITES RESERVED

1 TEASPOON VANILLA EXTRACT

1¼ CUPS SUGAR

½ CUP CAKE FLOUR

½ CUP UNSWEETENED COCOA POWDER

1 TEASPOON BAKING POWDER

6 TABLESPOONS (¾ STICK) UNSALTED BUTTER, MELTED

½ TEASPOON CREAM OF TARTAR

Preheat the oven to 350° F. Grease and flour a 9-inch springform pan. Line the bottom of the pan with parchment paper or wax paper. Grease the paper and set aside.

In a mixing bowl, beat the egg yolks on high speed for about 5 minutes, or until thick and lemon colored. Add the vanilla. Reduce the speed to low and gradually beat in 1 cup of the sugar. Continue beating until the mixture thickens slightly and doubles in volume, about 5 minutes.

In a small bowl, combine the cake flour, cocoa, and baking powder. Sift ⅓ cup of the flour mixture over the egg yolk mixture and fold it in until combined. Repeat with ⅓-cup measures of the remaining flour mixture until it is all incorporated. Blend in the melted butter.

In a mixing bowl, beat the egg whites and cream of tartar on medium speed until soft peaks form, about 2 minutes. Gradually add the remaining ¼ cup of sugar to the egg whites, beating on high speed until stiff peaks form. Gently fold 1 cup of the beaten egg white mixture into the egg yolk mixture to lighten the batter, then fold the whole yolk mixture into the egg white mixture. Pour into the prepared pan.

Bake for 25 to 35 minutes, or until the cake springs back when lightly touched. Cool on a wire rack for 10 minutes. Remove from the pan and cool completely.

SERVES 12

Sponge Cake

It's funny how the taste of a particular cake or the aroma of a freshly baked pie can transport us back in time. A woman I know tells me this cake brings back memories of growing up in Brooklyn in the 1920s and '30s. Every year, her birthday cake was a sponge cake topped with whipped cream and strawberries. She said when she tasted my sponge cake, it took her back sixty-five years. You can use this cake in many ways. Try it as the basis for Lemon Meringue Pie (page 118) or Triple Berry Tart (page 105). Or, like my friend, enjoy it topped with whipped cream, strawberries, and memories.

½ CUP CAKE FLOUR

1 TEASPOON BAKING POWDER

¼ TEASPOON SALT

3 EGGS SEPARATED, WHITES AND YOLKS RESERVED

⅓ CUP PLUS 3 TABLESPOONS SUGAR

½ TEASPOON ALMOND EXTRACT

3 TABLESPOONS (⅜ STICK) UNSALTED BUTTER, MELTED

¼ TEASPOON CREAM OF TARTAR

Preheat the oven to 350° F. Grease and flour a 9-inch springform pan. Line the bottom with parchment paper or wax paper. Grease the paper and set aside.

In a medium-size bowl, sift together the cake flour, baking powder, and salt.

In another mixing bowl, beat the egg yolks on high speed for about 4 minutes, or until thick and lemon colored. Gradually beat in ⅓ cup of the sugar and continue beating until the mixture thickens slightly and doubles in volume, about 4 minutes. Beat in the almond extract.

Sift half the flour mixture over the egg yolk mixture and fold it in until combined. Repeat with the remaining flour mixture. Blend in the melted butter.

In another mixing bowl, beat the egg whites and cream of tartar together on medium speed until soft peaks form. Gradually add the remaining 3 tablespoons of sugar, beating on high speed until stiff peaks form. Gently fold the egg whites into the batter.

Spoon the batter into the prepared pan. Bake for 14 to 16 minutes, or until the center springs back when lightly touched. Cool on a wire rack for 10 minutes. Remove from the pan and cool completely. This cake freezes well up to 3 months.

MAKES ONE THIN 9-INCH LAYER

NOTE: To make sponge cake crumbs, break the cake into pieces. In the bowl of a food processor, add the cake pieces and process, pulsing the machine on and off until the mixture turns to crumbs. Leftover cake crumbs freeze well for up to 3 months. One 9-inch sponge layer makes about 2½ cups of cake crumbs.

Baked Tart Crust

Our cookie-like tart crust makes an excellent foundation for any tart filling you can think of. Over the years we've filled it with custard, blueberry, strawberry, apple, lemon, honey-nut, and mousse fillings.

1 CUP PLUS 3 TABLESPOONS ALL-PURPOSE FLOUR

½ CUP CONFECTIONERS' SUGAR

¼ TEASPOON SALT

6 TABLESPOONS (¾ STICK) UNSALTED BUTTER,
    CUT INTO ½-INCH PIECES AND CHILLED

1 EGG YOLK

In the bowl of a food processor, blend together the flour, sugar, and salt. Add the butter and process, pulsing the machine on and off, until the mixture resembles very coarse meal. Add the egg yolk and process until moist clumps form. With your hands, gather the dough into a ball and flatten into a disk. Wrap the dough in plastic wrap and chill for 1 hour.

On a lightly floured work surface, roll out the dough into a 12-inch circle, about ⅛ inch thick. Transfer to 9-inch tart pan with a removable bottom. Press the dough gently into place, then trim the excess dough from around the edges. Freeze for 30 minutes.

Preheat the oven to 400° F. Line the crust with foil and fill it with dried beans or pie weights. Bake for 10 minutes. Remove the foil and the beans and reduce the oven temperature to 375° F. Bake for an additional 5 to 7 minutes, piercing it with a fork if the bottom bubbles. Cool the crust in the pan on a wire rack.

MAKES ONE 9-INCH TART SHELL

Pastry for Double-Crust Pie

*S*ure, *you can buy a ready-made piecrust, but a homemade one—especially this one—is so much more flaky and flavorful. For perfect results every time, make sure to chill the shortening well and use ice water. Use it for apple, peach, or berry pies.*

2 CUPS ALL-PURPOSE FLOUR

½ TEASPOON SALT

⅔ CUP VEGETABLE SHORTENING, CHILLED

6 TO 7 TABLESPOONS ICE WATER

In a medium mixing bowl, stir together the flour and salt. Using a pastry blender or two knives, cut in the shortening until the mixture crumbles into pea-size pieces. Add the water, 1 tablespoon at a time, blending with a fork until all the dough is moistened. Add more water if necessary. Divide the dough in half and form each half into a ball.

On a lightly floured surface, use your palm to slightly flatten one ball of dough. Using a floured rolling pin, roll the dough out from the center to the edge into a 12-inch circle.

To transfer the pastry to the pie plate, wrap it around a rolling pin. Unroll the pastry into a 9-inch pie plate. Ease the pastry into the pie plate, being careful not to stretch it. Add whatever filling you are using and trim the dough even with the rim of the pie plate.

Roll the remaining ball of dough into a 12-inch circle. Top the pie with the remaining crust, allowing a 1-inch overlap of top pastry around the edge. Fold the edge of the top crust under the bottom crust. Press well to seal and form a stand-up rim of pastry to flute. Flute as desired. Cut about eight 1-inch slits in the pastry to allow steam to escape. Bake as directed in individual recipes.

Pastry for Single-Crust Pie

*T*his tender, flaky pastry makes a great all-purpose pie dough. The rolling-pin transfer technique is an example of an old-time kitchen trick that still really works. This crust is ideal for pecan and meringue pies.

1 CUP ALL-PURPOSE FLOUR

½ TEASPOON SALT

⅓ CUP PLUS 1 TABLESPOON VEGETABLE SHORTENING, CHILLED

2 TO 3 TABLESPOONS ICE WATER

In a medium mixing bowl, stir together the flour and salt. Using a pastry blender or two knives, cut in the shortening until the mixture crumbles into pea-size pieces. Add the water, 1 tablespoon at a time, blending with a fork until all the dough is moistened. Add more water if necessary. Form the dough into a ball.

On a lightly floured surface, use your palm to slightly flatten the dough. Using a floured rolling pin, roll the dough from the center to the edge to form a 12-inch circle.

To transfer the pastry to a pie plate, wrap it around a rolling pin. Unroll the pastry into a 9-inch pie plate, being careful not to stretch it.

Trim the pastry to ½ inch beyond the edge of the pie plate. Fold the extra pastry under the rim and flute the edges as desired. Fill and bake as directed in individual recipes.

BAKED PASTRY SHELL: Prepare as above, except generously prick the bottom and sides of the pastry in the pie plate with a fork. Line the pastry with a double thickness of foil. Bake in a 450° F. oven for 8 minutes. Remove the foil. Bake 5 to 6 minutes more, or until golden brown. Cool on a wire rack.

Index